Beyond the Horizon

a travel memoir

Amazon Bestselling Author of
The Chausathi Yoginis of Hirapur and The Yoginis of Ranipur Jharial

Beyond the Horizon

a travel memoir

Dr. Adyasha Das

BLACK EAGLE BOOKS
Dublin, USA | BBSR, India
2022

Black Eagle Books
USA address:
7464 Wisdom Lane
Dublin, OH 43016

India address:
E/312, Trident Galaxy, Kalinga Nagar,
Bhubaneswar-751003, Odisha, India

E-mail: info@blackeaglebooks.org
Website: www.blackeaglebooks.org

First International Edition Published by
Black Eagle Books, 2022

BEYOND THE HORIZON
(a travel memoir)
by **Dr. Adyasha Das**

Copyright © Dr. Adyasha Das

All rights reserved. No part of this publication may be reproduced, stored in a retrieval system, or transmitted, in any form or by any means, electronic, mechanical, photocopying, recording or otherwise without the prior permission of the publisher.

Cover & Interior Design: Ezy's Publication

ISBN- 978-1-64560-090-9 (Paperback)
Library of Congress Control Number: 2022950571

Printed in the United States of America

Contents

Foreword	7
Of German Days and Indian Nights: **Germany**	17
A date with Mozart: **Austria**	63
The romance of Prague: **Czech Republic**	73
Walking with history at Quebec: **Canada**	76
Olive groves, gelato and a Roman Holiday: **Italy**	79
The Call of the Swiss Alps: **Switzerland**	89
The Shakespeare Trail: **England**	92
Loch Ness and Scottish Highlands: **Scotland**	95
Canyon roads and Vegas lanes: **United States**	102
The temples of the Gods: **Africa**	109
The mystic temples of Bagan: **Myanmar**	117
Vacation with the Filipinos: **Philippines**	126
Connecting to the past: **Cambodia**	130
A trip to Paradise: **Malaysia**	145
When the ruins speak: **Indonesia**	148

Foreword

Travel has been a life-long passion for me. I have been travelling ever since I can remember, for leisure and pleasure. Little did I know in my growing up years that I would join the travel and tourism world as a researcher and academician. All I knew as a child was that there was a beautiful world waiting to be discovered. It was a younger world then and I had plenty of time to unravel unknown roads and destinations. The fascination with travel probably began when I was a child. Childhood memories are precious and have had a profound impact on my life and creations. Memories of childhood are the dreams that we never forget. Whenever I walk down memory lane, I stop at this quaint gate, and a swarm of butterflies burst out in all their colour to paint my world with innocence, the honeysuckle smell of love dripping all over me. Those were the days of being unafraid of anything, everything because my parents held my hand. Far from being cloistered, I had the freedom to discover the beauty all around- the colourful butterflies that blew like flowers through the golden air, wild flowers with exotic names, and the diamond drops that rained and cleansed everything. My father was posted as an engineer at Dhenkanal a town in central Odisha and would take us along on his official trips. Those were fun trips for us. We were more interested for the jeep ride, the unknown roads and Ma's tasty food than the actual destination. I had no inkling then that those experiences were the beginning of several sojourns later in life.

My passion for travel continued in later years and I went on to see several destinations of the world as well as within the country that had existed only in books till that point of time. Some were planned trips but the most pleasant ones were those that just happened. Interestingly, I went on to teach and research on the psychology of travel behavior. As tourism comes of age, a greater number of people are realizing that their leisure and pleasure lies in undefined forms of tourism and travel. The new age traveler is redefining conventional market segments and revolutionizing the world of tourism products. The psychology of travel has touched all need levels identified by Maslow's theory of 'Need Hierarchy'.

As Pico Iyer states in an essay

"We travel, initially, to lose ourselves; and we travel, next, to find ourselves. We travel to open our hearts and eyes and learn more about the world than our newspapers will accommodate. We travel to bring what little we can, in our ignorance and knowledge, to those parts of the globe whose riches are differently dispersed. And we travel, in essence, to become young fools again — to slow time down and get taken in, and fall in love once more...."

There can thus be any number of travel motivations, from the most acceptable to the outright scandalous spurring people on to wander-lust: a break from routine, relaxation, antidote to stress, sun, sand and beach, recuperation / convalescence, health / fitness, family bonding, interpersonal relations, ethnic base, social networking, achievement orientation, status and prestige, self-discovery, cultural, education, professional / business, wanderlust.

The emerging travel trends include dominance of transformative travel trends and demands, new forms of Special Interest Tourism, alternative forms of tourism described as off-the-beaten-track tourism. Extension of cultural tourism leads to extending social horizons and tourists in search of 'authentic experience'.

Music tourism is travel directed towards particular authentic experiences, customized to the interests varying from traditional to contemporary musical interests against the back-drop of culture, arts, ethnic village life, paintings, visiting haunted castles or the like. It constitutes a cluster of possible tourists, activities, locations, attractions, workers and events which utilize musical resources for tourist purposes. The backpacker travel segment has burgeoned beyond imagination in recent times. With growing stress, nuclear and broken families, travel decisions are taken independently. Backpacking today is a style statement. The interpretation of one's identity and how we relate to destinations has undergone radical transformation. Travel is the dream-boat for the spiritual traveler or the healer.

Probably the earliest travelers were the nomadic hunters and food gatherers. They had no itinerary or plan to bind them. They travelled with the wind and the seasons, across deserts and forests and found food on the way. Australian aborigines, South African Bushmen, Pygmy Tribes of the Congo, Native Americans, and certain other tribes across the world are all variants of the nomadic migrant. They found shelter in caves and rock formations, depending on the natural environment. The essential difference was that they travelled in search of survival rather than leisure or identity. Since the earliest times of civilization, adventurous explorers have wandered far and wide in search of novelty. There were no travel blogs or guides for these daring travelers who dared enter dense jungles, confront dangerous animals, malaria infested regions, snowy avalanches or desert storms for the pleasure of knowing the unknown. The Hippie trail which started around the sixties brought forth the questioning traveler who set out for spiritual enlightenment, in search of God, identity or even solitude. The routes spanned from the cobbled stone ways of nondescript European villages to Asia's rich historical heritage, from the Silk route to Indian bazaars to Nepal's Buddhist monasteries. Travelers lived with the locals, ate their food and got to know their way of life.

Construction of Tourist Identity:

The new–age traveler is the one who questions everything he comes across and is swamped by self-doubt. Not for him the predictability of conventional travel patterns or living styles. In an attempt to redefine the self, the tourist

Maslow's need hierarchy

has become a popular cultural symbol of the recent times.

The tourist could travel for any or all of the need categories outlined by Maslow. Travel motivation is a blend of all these need categories, though they could also be focused on anyone of them. Travel motivations could span an entire gamut of needs: a desire to get away from the grind of life, a desire to know and see more, one's inner yearning for solitude and space.

Pearce applied Maslow's model of needs to tourism and combined it with the tourist's experience. He identified five layers of holiday motivations (from the bottom to the

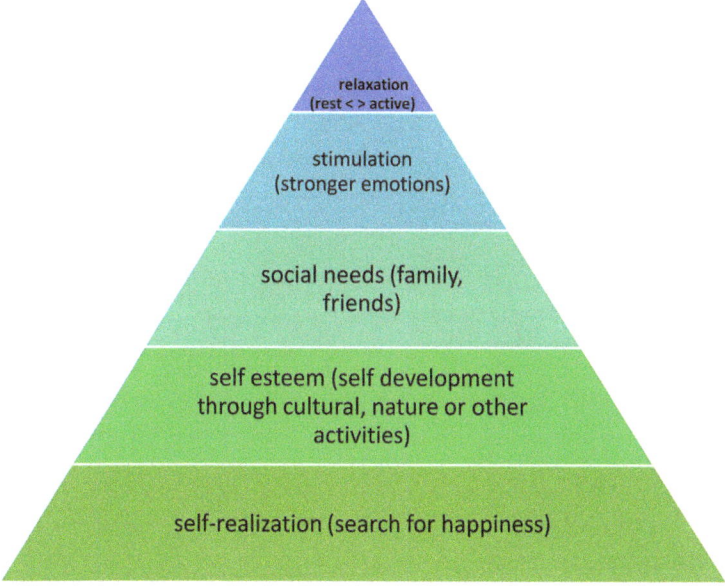

top of the pyramid):

Rejuvenation, exploration and relaxation are oft-quoted motives stimulating travel in this segment. The new age traveller is the one who is willing to negotiate identities. There is the need to redefine one's image. Meaningful identity constructions give meaning to the traveller's life. It is through symbolic consumption patterns through tourism that the traveller moulds his identity. As indicated by Ostergaard and Jantzen, in consuming tourism products and services, the traveller uses the fabric of emotions and feelings to create a coherent life. For the spiritual one's, travel experiences help in shaping the "self".

Often the consequence is an unintentional transformation of the self. There is also a state of inner bliss and self-actualization one attains in the process of self-identity creation. "Self-Fulfillment" is a state where travelers set out to achieve a personal goal/challenge and reflect upon accomplishment. "A musician must make music, an artist must paint, a poet must write, if he is to be ultimately happy. What a man can be, what he must be. This need we may call self-actualization" (Maslow).

The world has been, for most of us who like to travel and wander, a vast and difficult place to explore, an expensive proposition, and a path best traversed with friends. In India, it would mean travelling with family and staying with friends. However, the world has changed radically in the past few years. Smart phones and google have smartened the average traveler. The travel market in inundated with several new niche segments with a demand for new destinations.

Solo Travel is one of the noticeable travel trends in recent times in the tourism industry. Driven by transformations in social structures and changes in lifestyles, a fitter and more active aging population, the popularity of childless couples (DINK- Double income no kid) and late marriage, and especially the preference for being single have together resulted in noticeable changes in travel and leisure demands. Solo travel is partly driven by the fact that a major share of the population in developed countries and now, developing countries live in nuclear/single households. In India, the disintegration of the joint family system, the mass shift to urban areas and an increase in divorce rates have contributed to single living. This does not necessarily equate to a lonesome life (Danielson and Lohmann). An increasingly individualistic society and lack of connectedness are other factors encouraging solo travel.

Women travel solo for a plethora of reasons, ranging from the pleasure of travel to the very higher order wishes for self-actualization. Women travel to enjoy their own personal space and sometimes just to tick an item off the bucket list. The core motivations which influence decisions of women to travel solo are to experience the unknown, to rejuvenate the mind and self, to escape and as a part of the social fabric.

Solo travel has definite overlapping with creative and identity tourism. It leads to the creation of a new identity: the transition from an accompanying traveler to the sole traveler. Personal transformation in attempting to break free from gender stereotypes. Travelling solo triggers creativity in several ways. People seek escape from the routine of daily life in different ways which shape ever-new forms of special interest tourism. Towards the mid-life phase, most people travel to reinvent themselves, to rejuvenate mind and self. Creativity takes a leap when we open ourselves to new experiences, surroundings, expanded boundaries.

One significant element which plays a role in travel behaviour is identity. Desforges (2000) suggests that identity issues lie at the heart of our desire for travel. Highly mobile lifestyles are currently viewed as a positive identity marker. As outlined by Urry (2012), high mobility is associated with a high degree of 'meetingness', i.e., an individual's standing in society is reflected in mobility patterns, which ultimately necessitates air travel. This is also demonstrated through airlines' use of frequent flyer programmes which "reward and thus increase interest in mobility" (Gössling and Nilsson 2010, p. 242). Current literature relating to identities and tourism tends to focus on either 'finding yourself' through travel (e.g. Fullagar 2002; Noy 2004a) or using travel as a symbol of status (e.g. Thurlow and Jaworski 2006; Urry 2012).

Desforges (2000) suggests that understanding identity can give insight into tourism consumption because, by understanding the person and their needs and desires, it could be possible to predict their future travel behaviour. If the tourism identity processes an individual goes through could be understood, it might be possible to influence desired identities and consequently, travel behaviour. Culture and heritage lovers constitute yet another huge segment of travelers.

Cultural tourism is a segment of the tourism industry that is growing at an unprecedented pace as the trend towards specialized travel takes precedence. This trend is evident in the rising volume of tourists who seek adventure, culture, history, archaeology and interaction with local people (Hollinshead, 2004). Cultural tourism is one of the most significant global tourism markets. Culture and creative industries are being used most frequently to promote and popularize destinations and enhance their competitiveness and attractiveness. The world over, destinations are now focused on developing their tangible and intangible cultural assets to ensure a comparative advantage in an increasingly competitive tourism marketplace, and to create a prominent local distinctiveness in the face of globalization. Cultural heritage tourism is also gaining immense popularity among the new-age travelers. The neo-educated traveler breaks stereo-types and unravels his own travel needs and patterns.

Modern tourism, as well as consumption in general, is characterized by a high degree of individualization, flexibility and rapid changes. Identity has taken on a rather different meaning of differentiation, as difference has become the main objective of consumer choices, as mentioned by Rutherford (1990) and Baudrillard (1988), who suggest that people only buy goods to be different from others. This indicates that identity has come to contain elements of uniqueness rather than sameness to the individual. The personalities of solo travelers reflect similar considerations. An increasing number of tourists travel to discover themselves.

This book is a collection of experiences of my visits and travels to different destinations over time. It is a travel account, free from rules to travel writing and not a book of history. Needless to say, there are many more that will probably run into another volume. Special thanks to my family who have been constructive critics of my writings at all times. My sincere thanks to Sankar Narayan Mallik for his detailed inputs in editing this manuscript. His eye for detail and creative analysis has helped me immensely. I am thankful to Satya Pattanaik, Director, Black Eagle Books and Ashok Parida for their support in making this dream come true. I have been sharing these travel accounts as a serial in social media. The interest and appreciation of my readers made me contemplate the idea of putting it together in the form of a book.

Of German Days and Indian Nights

FRANKFURT

Frankfurt am Main

    The blurred faces of my family members who had come to see me off became indistinct as I bid good bye to them and took one step closer to Germany. From the window of the aircraft, the grandeur of my homeland, Odisha, moved me. The clean air, green coconut trees, with their silhouette in the ponds and above all, the simple people – an unforgettable combination. But I had been amidst all this my whole life. What was especially breath-taking today? Or was it that distance extinguished commonplace passions and increased great ones, just as the wind extinguished candles and kindled fire?

My mind travelled back to my first sojourn to Germany, as a part of touring Europe with my family. The travel agent had ingenuously called it the "Maaza" experience. Maaza translates as fun, but the magic of the Rhine far surpassed the limits of the word fun and cascaded into the realms of an ethereal experience. In that first trip, from Schaffhausen we had travelled onwards to view the majestic Rhine falls, and then crossed the German border to enter a zone of timeless beauty and unparalleled scenery – the Black Forest region. Though the pine trees were more green than black, there were deep, impenetrable shadows amidst them that stretched out to me. It was almost as if the little dwarfs and goblins there were whispering, 'Come back again'! The small idyllic villages and cuckoo clocks at Freiburg have remained etched in my mind. I had stayed at Mannheim before going to Cologne for marvelling at Europe's largest Gothic twin spire cathedral: 'Dom'. I had been awestruck at the way beauty and architecture had been interwoven. An unforgettable cruise on River Rhine flanked on both sides with unforgettable views of mysterious mountains, fairy tale castles and fortresses from a bygone era, all these images, in a nutshell was the way I had first seen Germany and was intrigued enough to want to go back.

When I had first learned about my selection for the 'Akshar writer-in-residence' program at Germany, I was thrilled. And then I pondered about Akshar, the letter which teams up with others to form words, the power a word contains to reach out beyond geographical boundaries and connect people, places, passions. Words, to talk about light, shades and hues, across centuries, their fiery expressiveness. Words to convey the whispers of wild flowers, mountains, human bodies – words in a transcendental language of the senses. I looked forward to my game with words, in the backdrop of Frankfurt, to use them to whisk me off to India whenever I wanted and in a moment be back in my new home, almost like building a bridge of words between the two countries. I had already read up on Frankfurt and had seen the imposing white pillars of the Frankfurt Literature House on the internet. I wanted to explore everything- the streets, the museums, people, alone-ness, loneliness, moods, getting lost, finding myself again.

> Like a gentle breeze of words,
> Lost in it on a calm morning,
> A chance meeting with it on a dusky evening,
> In a single moment,
> To gather up all my thoughts
> And offer this affair with Frankfurt,
> My words.

The flight was on time. The aerial view of Frankfurt was strangely familiar. Have I visited this place before? In my dreams or in some earlier birth? Perhaps my poetry has traversed through ages, like some age-old sea, a torrential Indian river steering its course to Frankfurt. It will reject nothing it can collect in its course – passion, mystery and the hearts of the Germans. Martina Kigle, intern at the Frankfurt Literature House, was at the airport to receive me. Almost immediately after the cab started, she pointed out the elegant skyscrapers and towers characterizing Frankfurt. A hub of international business, finance, and trade fairs as well as host to the largest airport in the continent, Mainhattan as it is popularly referred to (The Main River flows through

Frankfurt), is also a city of art and culture. Frankfurt am Main is a statement of unmistakable contradictions. The traditional and the modern, big city bustle and tranquility, all happily co-exist.

I had been provided with a lovely apartment, Liv'In Frankfurt. Bright yellow walls, matching curtains and a big picture window with a terrific view of the skyline of Frankfurt. A home away from home, in the place where the poet Johann Wolfgang von Goethe lived and thought. Completely alone, with my words and thoughts. Man is a social animal. I remember a long time back, in the Sociology classes at college, this line had been droned into our heads. So, in being social I had invited few others to live with me, despite my self-proclaimed solitary status. My daughter smiled at me from the picture on my table. My family members walked out of the memories I had carried so carefully across the miles, and had spread out all over the apartment. But mostly there were strangers in my room. I had collected a basketful of smiles of strangers. Some specially for me, others quizzically, carelessly flung across rooms, but mostly, I had picked up the ones that were left uncared for on the streets, along the banks of the River Main.

In the afternoon, I visited the Literaturhaus Frankfurt. It was a regal building with beautiful white pillars. During World War-II, Frankfurt was heavily bombed and its medieval city center was destroyed. The mansion housing the Literaturhaus Frankfurt was reduced to rubble, except those colossal white pillars which had been mute witness to the tears and pain of thousands of innocents. They say stones sometimes speak out dark secrets, like the statue of Memnon in

Egypt. As I passed the pillars, I pressed my ears against one of them. There was not even a faint whisper. Perhaps it was shy. I remembered the refrains of a song:

> Edelweiss, Edelweiss,
> every moment you greet me
> Small and white, clean and bright,
> you look happy to meet me

I knew the pillars were greeting me, as they had welcomed writers of many nationalities. I went on a short tour of the Haus and was immediately struck by the atmosphere of congeniality and friendliness. The primary goal of the Literaturhaus is to present the different nuances and subtleties of literature to all people. There was an ongoing exhibition on the life and works of Robert Walser, 1878-1956. I saw many manuscripts filled with a remarkable handwriting. I saw the simple life he had led in the recreation of his room, and finally his death in the snow that he had so deeply admired. He had suffered, had had a liberal share of triumphs and defeats. As I came out I paid my tribute to the great author:

> When you hold the pen, the lines dance,
> When you write, the words shimmer,
> When you paint, the colours sing.
> So all things have
> meaning in that space beyond time where you are now.

In the evening, at 8 p.m. there was a reading by noted writer Peter Stamm in the Literaturhaus auditorium. An impressive venue, packed to the brim. I had never realized that anonymity could be so enjoyable.

Floating in and out of the vast rooms of the Haus, not knowing a single soul, but not minding in the least bit. No compulsion to be sociable, to talk merely because convention forbids silence, to rub against each other in order to create the illusion of intimacy.

German, as a language, is musical. The gentleman at the podium had an excellent style of communication. The audience was listening with rapt attention. Peter Stamm came on next and spoke music, I mean German in a different way. Almost like the musical ragas in Indian music, which portray human feelings and emotions of varied patterns through the interplay of notes. I can definitely say that the audience had a few inattentive listeners, trying to look every bit alert. Probably caught in a cobweb of thoughts about an appointment to be kept, some problem at home, or even thinking about me. The only woman in the room dressed differently, not understanding a word of German except Frau and yet every bit the avid fan.

Literaturhaus, Frankfurt

Latte macchiato in Frankfurt

Latte macchiato was the fascinating name of the coffee I had yesterday at the Haus. A tall cup with a sea of froth to be scooped up with a spoon for taste, and beneath that, the coffee. It is a bit bitter, yet sweet. Just like life. A lonely flame surrounded by a womb of many coloured lights. Like peace – when prolonged bitterness has been washed away by tears. Like realization, a white cloud glittering over the murmuring forest of books. There are many places in the metropolis along the River Main where one can enjoy the pleasures of the city's coffee scene. Frankfurt's coffeehouses are as diversified as the city itself with a coffee culture that is traditional, international, original and experimental!

I had been looking around at other apartments near mine, whatever I could see from the lights burning in the windows. It had been a childhood curiosity to look at windows of unknown houses and imagine the lives lived there, of course always imagining 'and-they-lived-happily-ever-after' endings. All windows were pretty and had a distinguishing character, with delicate lace curtains fluttering unhurriedly, or small patios laden with bright, flirtatious flowers. I had mostly seen the elderly people, in the kitchen or lazing in the balcony, but on their own, as if counting the days before the final journey.

Each day I would set out to explore a bit of Frankfurt. The traffic was much less than in India and very controlled. Every now and then I would ask my friend Martina, 'Do you think this is a crowded street'? She would say yes and I would wonder at the emptiness. In my walks down unknown streets and roads, I encountered unique combinations of old, historic buildings and modern skyscrapers. I reminisced about the time I had spent in Manhattan, New York, and the ambitious skyscrapers were very similar. Frankfurt was an unpredictable beauty – full of old world charm one minute and chic and suave the next. I saw the famous banks for which Frankfurt was popularly referred to as Bankfurt – The Eurotower, Dresdner Bank, Commerzbank, Deutsche Bank and Citibank. All towers were in competition to reach out and touch the sky, like birds perched upon a tremendous cliff. The Opernplatz street was famous for the Altes Opernhaus. In the square, water gushed out of the Marschallbrunnen, as though it was too tired of company and tried to be far from the madding crowd.

We followed the footpath through the Taunusanlage and proceeded on to Gallusanlage. I felt a magic wand had touched us and we were all at once in the countryside. I was pleasantly surprised to spot this green belt amidst the concrete jungle; low trees, their soft, silky leaves swaying in the light breeze. My feet sank into the cushion of dead

leaves. The pigeons were gathered to bask in the sun. I had an uncanny feeling that someone was staring at me. I looked up to see the Goethe memorial in the park. I walked up to him and stood close. Since the time I had known him, our relationship had reached a point where I never expected a response. I could understand his silence. His poetry, words, sounds, like pretty butterflies buzzed past me.

From the 54th floor of the Main Tower, with a height of 205m, I viewed the majestic sight of Frankfurt leisurely spread out on all sides. I had a fear of heights. Atop Eiffel Tower in Paris and Sears Tower in Chicago, I had stayed away from the edge. On a crisp, starched curtain, the faintest streak of dirt is prominent. At such heights, a moment's indulgence may mean endless possibilities of death. Do you know the story of the master window-washer? After doing a superb job of cleaning windows on the 110th storey of the Chicago Tower, he made the mistake of stepping back to admire his work. Such awe-inspiring moments only remind about the Creator and his canvas, on which I was a very small speck of colour.

I had seen quite a few Indians on the streets, along with people of other nationalities. Frankfurt appeared to me a multi-cultural pot-pourri. We entered an Indian store and I bought some groceries. My friend Martina commented that I looked more relaxed and at home there. The shop was crammed with various items and along with the smell of incense sticks the unmistakable flavour of India wafted in the air. Leisurely strolling along the streets with all the time in the world, and a bag full of Indian groceries, I felt happy. The pavements were clean. I could not resist indulging in window-shopping - breathtaking porcelain and exquisitely crafted jewellery in the shops along Goethe strasse. Jewellery for all moods-Bracelets with a blazing eloquence for silent afternoons, sparkling beams from diamond-studded ear-rings to light up dark nights; the melody of a necklace for sudden streaks of naughtiness. Shyness attempting liberation in the language of pearls.

We moved on to a small restaurant, 'DoyDoy' in Kaiser street, the bridge between the main station and the inner city and also the Rotlichtviertel – the red-light district. The chairs strewn casually under the awnings overlooking the streets reminded me so much of the Champs d' Elysée in Paris; where Victor Hugo and Anais Nin spent sleepy, satin evenings, where I had visited with stars in my eyes and came back with wine in them. Where over cheese and wine, writers would discuss how their poetry was born like a hill-brook and how, like the rain, their works had several tones. I used the tram system, the Straßenbahn as well as the U-bahn for getting around.

Sometimes opportunity knocks, but most of the time it sneaks up and then quietly steals away. Before that happened I wanted to befriend this opportunity to know Frankfurt! My six honest serving men would assist me. What, Why, When, How, Where and Who.

Trying to drown a shy Sunday afternoon in the Main was a favourite leisure activity. The Main River looked to be many things. It was magnanimous, a slow waltz of erotic twists and turns, bedecked with dazzling white boats, the star- speckled sky a loyal and bemused spectator. The Frankfurt 'Messen', or trade fairs brought travellers and traders from far and wide plying up and down the Main with their merchandise. The legend goes that Emperor Charlemagne and his troops were hounded by their enemies and were desperately trying to flee. They reached a dead-end when they arrived at the banks of the Main, which appeared to be a labyrinth of meandering waterways and islands. Lady Luck smiled at them in the form of a doe that led them to a ford which carved a safe passage across the Main. The river had thus had a significant role to play in Frankfurt's development.

The Sachsenhausen stretch of the main embankment has around eight museums and is also known as the 'Museumsufer'. I often took a walk along the river and viewed the palatial buildings that housed these museums. On enquiring I learned that these mansions were once built by aristocratic families and now belonged to the city. Seated on a wooden bench in front of the Städelsches Kunstinstitut, I admired its architecture. When Johann F. Städel created a foundation with stable financial support and a huge collection of rare paintings and books that he had collected, a tiny Städel was born. Today it boasts an impressive collection of European masterpieces and sculptures, rare gems created by Rubens, Beckmann, Picasso etc. Pictures have a power that is renewed constantly. They converse with their viewers in silence and have a special message for each of them. The muted lighting and the layer of silence shrouding the interiors was a perfect ambience for my meeting with the great masters. Schmidt-Rotluff's 'Im Kiosk' revealed a very different artistic approach. The amber in Lovis Corinth's ' Walchensee in Winter' made me drunk. Painting, like poetry, is a miracle. A literary or painting career may fetch accolades, bring the most elusive fame to one's doorstep, or even bring monetary rewards. But I believe what happens to me when I write is much more important.

I loved going on walking tours of Frankfurt, leisurely strolls through the unknown streets. Because the city is so compact, walking is one of the most enjoyable ways to look around. Away from the exhibition, down the posh locality of Bertramstrasse, the houses were straight out of Grimm's fairy-tales, with neat, well - tended gardens laden with bright blooms. The lace curtains at the windows were expensive, with fine designs. At times, there were rare curios or vases adorning the window-sills. In these lanes, petals of sweet-scented flowers filled the air, music blew along in the breeze. A quiet, drowsy neighbourhood led to the Dornbusch railway station, and I fell in love with it. We chose a restaurant with a name full of Gold – 'Goldener Adler' with cozy chairs and tables strewn casually, right next to a medieval street, under a canopy of trees. As the leaves of memory rained on us, of Frankfurter's family and food of yester-years, we placed the order.

The German Apfelwein, popularly nicknamed Ebbelwein in Frankfurt dialect, had been recommended. The German adaptation of apple cider (aka *apfelwein*, *ebbelwei, ebbelwoi, schoppe,* or *stöffsche*) is the beloved of all Frankfuters and there is a dedicated pitcher and glass for serving it in each home.

I choose a Süßgespritzter, a heady combination of apple wine and lemonade. Goethe's favourite 'Grüne Sosse', a sauce of at least seven finely chopped herbs (parsley, chives, chervil, sorrel, dill, borage, tarragon, lorage and a lemon-flavoured herb- Zitronenmelisse.) poured over chopped, hard – boiled eggs and boiled potatoes. To be very truthful, I had been a bit apprehensive about the taste. I have had earlier experiences to prove that appearances can be deceptive, especially in a foreign land. It was most delectable and pleasing to the eye, though new to my taste – buds. There is a famous myth that green sauce was Johann Wolfgang von Goethe's favourite dish, originally created by his mother. Locals love to connect their favourite fare with the celebrated author, who was born in Frankfurt. In reality, the recipe of Frankfurter Grüne Soße was published for the very first time in a cookbook by Wilhelmine Rührig in 1860, 30 years after the death of Goethe.

Romance in the flea market

I remember some lines of Wordsworth which I always found universally true:

My heart leaps up when I behold a rainbow in the sky
So was it when my life began
So is it now I am a man
So be it when I shall grow old...

    I have always been a die-hard romantic. From sandcastles along the beach to sullen moments, spinning drunken fantasies with gossamer threads of dreams, Mozart, Bach, Beethoven, long telephone calls in the wee hours, browsing for hours in antique shops, reminiscing the past, dog-eared, sepia-coloured. Of course I know, the past is enticing and perfect because it is more truly our creation than anything else. We recreate the past, chiselling and moulding it to a perfectly desired shape; remember only what we want to, adding clever repartees which were unspoken then. But oh! That sighing at the pimply youth, a touch, a forbidden kiss, a stray summer madness.

    The Flea Market in Frankfurt has been going on for many a year. Every Saturday, people would gather along the Main riverbank beginning at the Eisener Steg bridge and buy and sell to their heart's delight. A few years ago, it began switching locations every other week. I had an appointment with unknown pasts, in the flea market. From quite a distance, I could feel its pulse, see the vibrant colours. I was awe-struck! On the banks of the Maine, hundreds of stalls had been put up, almost like an Indian bazaar. There were varieties of items – old clothes, household appliances, antique furniture. There was a liberal sprinkling of the traditional Apfelwein (cider) pubs on that side of the river, to revitalize weary shoppers. There was quite a crowd of eager shoppers and I loved the fun-fair feel of the place. I got stuck at each stall, mesmerized by the uncommon combination of wares – movie posters, paintings, African sculptures, books, old Russian cameras, Charleston dresses, Indian bead necklaces, Chinese dolls, the list was endless.

My eyes were drawn to some rare curios, exquisitely crafted and I stopped in my tracks, something which I had been doing quite often that day. Those items must have belonged to a house amidst flower-strewn pastures and whispering forests. The lady of the house must have been proud of the bright red geraniums in her window box. The man would of course have had that old-world chivalry and would have travelled far and wide to collect and gift her the curios.

I spotted a half-used perfume bottle; the amber coloured liquid immediately brought to mind a languid river coursing through sun-dappled woods and brooks. Who had used it? When? Flashing knives, probably brandished by warring knights in Dinkelsbühl, Nordlingen or Rothenburg. Stone-studded dainty boxes gifted to sweetheart. The moment I held them in my palm, the air took on the heady fragrance of a rose garden. I was probably holding the key to a mysterious love story. Lovely art lamps, with silver and bronze designs fit for a king. Crystal and porcelain with exotic designs. Quaint wooden boxes of a bygone era. And Yeats' immortal lines, captured in an exquisitely patterned carpet, a dream.

I have spread my dreams under your feet, Tread softly as you tread on my dreams.

How had such precious things been given away? What had happened to the relationships around which these had been gathered? Or is it that once in a while, one gives away things to make place for new ones – new furniture, paintings, relationships? As we were about to leave, my eyes were riveted on a doll, beckoning me with innocent, blue eyes, a shock of yellow hair parted on both sides into two neat pony tails. Somewhere, sometime, tender hands must have held it and clutched it to the chest, a baby voice must have crooned a hundred loving names. With childhood gone and in the effervescent growing up years, the doll had probably been forgotten and given away. I bought it and it is now sitting on my table looking prettier.

I can now weave a beautiful tapestry of romance, based on a wild 'Rheingau' affair and a German doll for an Indian Home.

The Main, Moon and Me

The Encyclopaedia Britannica states:

'Latin Moenus, river, an important right (East) bank tributary of the Rhine in Germany; formed near the Kulmbach, by the confluence of the Weisser (White) Main, which rises in the Fichtel Mountains and the Roter (Red) Main.'

I have lost a very close friend; we had promised each other we would hold hands and walk. The banks of the Main can be very crowded with the rush of revellers on the weekend. Somehow my clasp loosened and my confidante slipped away. So elusive was my friend, could be anywhere; in the cafes dotting the Main on both its sides, the wooden benches sprawling in the sun or even in the Main itself. Oh Tranquillity, where are you?

I told you, my friend can remain incognito anywhere, everywhere, a lull of mellow September nights in the midst of concrete, the smell of honeysuckle. There in the mirror-world of the shimmering Main was my friend, Tranquillity.

I was trying my very best to drown that shy Sunday afternoon in the Main. The Frankfurt 'Messen', or trade fairs brought travellers and traders from far and wide plying up and down the Main with their merchandise. The legend goes that Emperor Charlemagne and his troops were hounded by their enemies and were desperately trying to flee. They reached a dead-end when they arrived on the banks of the Main, which appeared to be a labyrinth of meandering waterways and islands. Lady Luck smiled at them in the form of a doe that led them to a ford that carved a safe passage across the Main. The river has thus had a significant role to play in Frankfurt's development.

The illustrious past of Frankfurt is captured in some forty museums, many of which are clustered about the Main River bank. It had been unusually warm those days and I saw many bikers skirting the Main, daring the sun for a tan. On the north side of the river was a cycle path that ran along the river for more than 30 km. Sitting there, I enjoyed the beautiful scenery and got an insight into Sunday celebrations by the locals. There were young couples, kissing under an unexpected drizzle, ecstatically indifferent to both propriety and puddles, families squeezed into the small cafes. The lush green parks dotting the river bank offered unending stretches of jogging trails, far from the madding crowd. Several bridges spanned the length of the Main, iron networks of connectivity. I posed for a photo on the Eiserner Steg, a pedestrian bridge, and my mind flew to similar bridges, familiar waters I had encountered elsewhere.

My cruise on the Seine which revealed Paris as a city steeped in romance, delicious dishes and wine to wash it down in boulevard brasserie or London in all its splendour displayed around the Thames – from the Victorian iron work to Big Ben, and of course the strong old bridges on which I had spent an eternity. An unforgettable canal cruise and the Amstel river in Holland, Holy Ganges back home, the Mahanadi of my own Odisha and my mysterious Nile on whose shadowy banks I had had a secret tryst with Tutankhamen. Cities have been built on the banks of life-giving rivers, have been washed away in their fury; but rivers have been indispensable.

Standing on the Iron Bridge atop the Main I heard the melodious strains of a young boy playing the accordion, almost painful in its beauty, heart-rending in its melody. I remembered Aldous Huxley's line...'After silence, that which comes nearest to expressing the inexpressible is music.' I felt sublime. Isn't life like a river? Musically gurgling across time? Just as it's impossible to hold a moonbeam in our hands, our time on Earth flows out of childhood pranks, onwards to a euphoric youth and before one knows it, the pace slows down, the work is done and it is time to go. Time has been instigating me to yearn for the next day, next year, to gallop ahead. But no. I have forced it to a halt here. All that matters is the present, that moment as the Main turned into gold in the twilight and life in Frankfurt flowed in a heady mixture of happiness and courage.

So rested the Main between its banks, silently serenaded by the moon in loyal tenderness. As I looked up, the moon showered down a misty sheet of tears, tears that would become dewdrops in the parks the next morning.

A book called Frankfurt

Books have been my companions since as far back as I can remember. Channel television had not intruded into my life when I entered the fascinating world of books. My imagination would race with the horizon, daring to out-smart it. I remember my parents collecting books from all over – Shakespeare, Charles Dickens, Wordsworth, Byron, famous as well as lesser-known poets and writers, all were invited into my small library at home. Tolstoy, Chekov and later Pablo Neruda, Quasimodo, Marquez -from these great masters I learned to open the windows of my mind. I learned to dream. Books of all kinds, colours, sizes enticed me to dream of other worlds, nature, to connect with each other and with our better selves. I perceived reading as a way to move further up in the journey to wisdom – from the yearnings of youth to a growing desire to understand life's larger purposes. So I wanted to visit a bookshop here in Frankfurt. The Carolus Buchhandlung was a bookstore with a difference. Neat rows of books were arranged in wooden shelves. A great variety of books – some to answer the biggest questions of life, books on several disciplines, few to colour the innocent world of a child. Most of the books were in German and I was only able to recognize the names of authors. A quaint edition of a masterpiece of the great Columbian story– teller, Gabriel Garcia Marquez, ' One Hundred Years of Solitude', illustrated chronicles of Frankfurt etc. I found stacks of words, dressed in their best. Long after I returned, that month long stay in Frankfurt remained throbbing and alive, in similar rows of words contained within velvet covers.

  I had an afternoon appointment with Nicole, from the online version of the Frankfurt General Newspaper at the restaurant MOLOKO overlooking the Main. There was a breeze coming up from the river and a naughty drizzle sneaking up behind us. I saw, yet again, many old – timers, alone or with their dogs, enjoying a jug of wine. Long – standing low birth rates and increasing life-expectancy had resulted in Germany having the third – largest proportion of elderly people world – wide. In fact, approximately every fourth person was old there. Our conversation steered to India, the culture and folkways, languages and dialects and literary trends in poetry and fiction, the changing social and literary situation and how it influenced my writings.

We discussed about certain similar patterns in German and Indian writing – exploration of the experience of love in all its richness, complexity and variety, the subtleties and nuances of individual sensibility, an obsession with the self, often in philosophical and existential frames and, of course, a simmering concern with historical themes.

Undoubtedly, Indian poetry and fiction increasingly projects a woman – centred approach, to interpret and project experience from the viewpoint of a feminine consciousness and sensibility. As we walked back, Martina, my constant companion, told me it was safe for women to go around late at night. I had felt very comfortable going for a stroll in the evenings. Even in my 'salwar – kameez', my typical Indian attire, I didn't invite unnecessary stares. Tremendous progress has been made in Germany in 'equal rights' for women and they now account for 45 percent of all employed persons. As I approached Lange Strasse, the streets were quieter though familiar. Everyone was in a hurry, briskly walking towards an unknown destination. I realized why I didn't feel alone there. Even as a child, in the densely forested world of books, I had never been afraid to be the lone traveller. I had always liked the adventure of being on my own, figuring out meanings without knowing them. Many times, in my journey into books, I would get lost. There would be mountainous terrains on which I would lose my foothold and hang precariously. The roaring sea would threaten to drown me. But soon the danger would be past; the sea would become an endless ribbon of caresses and I would march ahead with a new confidence. The spire of the ' Imperial Cathedral', the Kaiserdom, was the silent sentry ensuring that all is well. As the lights started twinkling in the skyscrapers, the laser-beams of the FFH radio on the top of the head office of Frankfurt Commerzbank, I realized every bit of Frankfurt reverberated with life, for the proper function of life was to live, not to exist.

> I agreed with the philosophy of Frankfurt.
> I would rather be ashes than dust.
> I would rather be a superb meteor,
> every atom of me in magnificent glow
> than a sleepy and perseverant planet.

I would rather have my spark burn out in a brilliant blaze than be stifled by dry rot. For the proper function of life is to live, not to exist.

Passion in the Theatre

The opening ceremony of the Festival of Literature – 'Literaturm' (literatower), was being organised by the City of Frankfurt at the Literature House. The festival's main theme was the Poetry of Knowledge – Die Poesie des

Wissens. The front row was packed with distinguished Who's Who of Frankfurt. Amidst the flashing of cameras, Petra Roth, the mayor, initiated the program with her address. There were scholars, writers, bureaucrats - and I could sense from their body language that the audience was seriously attentive. 'Poetry is a revelation of words by means of words', the words of George Steiner. He spoke emphatically and the audience cheered him on. Durs Grünbein read a poem aloud and then they had an animated discussion. I couldn't follow the dialogue, but I gathered it was a discussion on literature and science, science and art, and novels pertaining to scientific issues.

I was impressed with the efficient organization and team – work of everyone at the Literature House. The head of the house, Dr. Maria Gazzetti, had left town on some urgent personal work. But I met her briefly on my first day there. Of course there was Maike Zeidler, chic and elegant, who is a good friend. In between her preoccupations, we had snatched some moments to have fleeting discussions on astrology and the teachings of Bhagwan Rajneesh or Osho, master of rhetoric who took the world by storm when he proclaimed that the body precedes the mind in importance when it comes to spiritual enlightenment.

That evening, we visited the Schauspiel, Frankfurt, Frankfurt's Theatre, to see Heiner Müller's ' Quartett'. It was very thoughtful of Maike and Martina to have organized it at my request. I had read that German drama either focussed on comedy or was tragic, like the one I was seeing that night. I was reminded of Goethe's Faust where the hero's love was his salvation. The play that day was an adaptation of the novel 'Dangerous Love' by the 18th century French author Laclos. The war of sexes, the embittered love between Marquise de Merteuil and

Vicomte de Valmont, it was a complicated saga of human passion beautifully depicted in the short one – hour play by Urs Troller and Adriane Westerbarkey. Eric Berne, in his best – seller, 'Games People Play' talks about unpredictable human transactions. Individuals use their three ego – states, (parent, adult and child) to play psychological games with one another. There has been a liberal use of psychology in theatre and literature. The scenes that were enacted were powerful articulations of passion. From the Freudian perspective, human passion is laden with dark intimations. Lorca defined the passionate streaks in poems as 'duende ', a sheer madness that burns the blood of Vicomte de Valmont and drives the Marquise to the very edge of reality. How can a relationship become so bitter and bring out the worst in a person? The quicksilver smudges of melancholy, loneliness and lunacy, desire and death were effectively portrayed by the actors. As we returned through the deserted by-lanes, I recollected Neruda's lines that aptly sum up the Quartett:

> Well, now,
> If little by little you stop loving me
> I shall stop loving you little by little.
> If suddenly you forget me
> Do not look for me
> For I shall already have forgotten you.

I missed home, and those "miss – you" moments appeared suddenly and took me by surprise. The new sights and sounds, behaviour- and eating-patterns, concepts of personal space, norms and values had crowded my mind, instilling excitement and enthusiasm. I found euphoria all around and within me. Some friends had warned that soon the magic would wear off and there would be inevitable confusion and disorientation. They had asked me to remove my rose – tinted sunglasses. But I found the colour did not lie in my glass. It was everywhere outside and I couldn't help walking into that haze.

Frankfurt was holding my hand and I wanted to be led everywhere, into hubs of people, brimming streets, coy cafes, proud churches, theatre, opera , banks, towers. I wanted to be led everywhere.

Of German Days and Indian Nights

It has been an unusually warm autumn, they said. For a change, the weather had not been very temperamental and there was wonderfully warm weather and brilliant blue skies. The Frankfurters were utilizing this rare spell of honey – gold weather in the best way possible, skating, cycling, and sun – bathing on the banks of a cheerful Main. That lazy Sunday I had a free day...to prepare myself for a special evening, the Indische Nacht – The Indian Night. I had been invited to read my poems and perform some songs along with other famous Indian writers: Kiran Nagarkar, Gagan Gill and Shafi Shauq.

Ever since I can remember, I have been passionate about music and have been an ardent fan of the great masters. Music is the manifestation of human spirit, similar to language. Its greatest practitioners have conveyed to mankind things not possible to say in any other language. Like literature, music is a part of everyone's life, whether it is just entertainment, a cultural expression or religious inspiration. It has been found to have a profound effect on our physiological and psychological well – being.

> William Congreve wrote:
> 'Music hath charm to soothe the savage breast,
> to soften rocks, or bend a knotted oak,

I have read that things inanimate moved,
And as with living souls have been informed,
By magic numbers and persuasive sound.'

Music therapy interventions are now being increasingly designed to manage stress, alleviate pain, promote wellness, express feelings, enhance memory, improve communication and promote physical rehabilitation the world over. Music has the power to explore the realms that cannot be accessed with words. Some of my all time favourites have coincidentally been German composers...Johann Sebastian Bach, one of the greatest Baroque composers. Beethoven's mysterious creations and especially his moonlight sonata and Concerto, an ultimate trial for all music lovers. Brahms immortal church music and symphonies... Richard Wagner who considered himself to be 'the most German of men' and celebrated the German way of life in his music.... But I have a confession to make. Despite my immense regard for all the maestros, I have been in love for as long as I can remember with only one, Wolfgang Amadeus Mozart....whose melodies have spanned the distance from the sublime to the stupendous, melancholic to happy. Oh! How I have rambled on. Let me get back to the Indian Night. The main organizer of the event was Mr. Peter Ripken who had contacted me earlier and I was very impressed with his planned approach, from rehearsals to translations of the works to be presented. Sonja Vandenrath, a most accomplished lady had also been in touch regarding this program. The dusky evening arrived and we were in the auditorium. When I observed the details of preparation, from the order of seating on the dias to voice testing, I was in awe. The doors opened at seven and the hall filled up with an enthusiastic audience.

A hall full of Germans to savour a flavour called India. The moderator, Holger Ehling had a most pleasant style and was an intelligent host, linking the whole program together with clever repartee.

There was Indian decor, food and people who said they could feel the pulse of my Odia songs. Women and men who encouraged me and proved what I had always known: music communicates across cultures, overcoming barriers of language. Indian art, whether it is painting, poetry, dance or music has a characteristically inward quality...a manifestation of the world – view of this culture. Indian thought, at its deepest, affirms that mind and matter are rather different grades of the same energy, different organizations of one conscious force of existence.

Music, as well as being the most dispensable of arts, is probably the hardest to throw off. Just as memories and landscapes eventually emerge to make emotional claims upon us, music comes uninvited. And stays. It is the lure of place, the call to belong. That evening, music and literature combined to create an unforgettable symphony called 'German days and Indian nights'.

The author with eminent poets Shafi Shauq and Gagan Gill at Indische Nachtim Mousonturm, Frankfurt

A Miracle called Städel

The Sachsenhausen stretch of the main embankment has around eight museums and is also known as the 'Museumsufer'. I often took a walk along the river and viewed the palatial buildings that housed the museums. On enquiring I learned that the mansions were once built by aristocratic families and now belonged to the city. I liked sitting on the wooden bench in front of the Städelsches Kunstinstitut. When Johann F. Städel created a foundation with stable financial support and a huge collection of rare paintings and books that he had collected, a tiny Städel was born. Today it boasts an impressive collection of European masterpieces and sculptures. I had a strong desire to see these rare gems created by Rubens, Beckmann, Picasso etc. But I also felt an eagerness to discover something new. Pictures have a power that is renewed constantly. They converse with their viewers in silence and have a special message for each of them. The muted lighting and the layer of silence shrouding the interiors was a perfect ambience for my meeting with the great masters. Schmidt-Rotluff's 'Im Kiosk' revealed a very different artistic approach. The amber in Lovis Corinth's' Walchensee in Winter' made me drunk. Painting, like poetry, is a miracle. A literary or painting career may fetch accolades, bring the most elusive fame to one's doorstep, or even bring monetary rewards. But I believe what happens to me when I write is much more important.

Any creative effort, be it Vincent Van Gogh's brilliant musings on canvas, or Mozart's aching symphonies, or Rilke's poetry, is about becoming a human being. Not creating something, but creating ourselves. If you ask me what is so special about Arnold Bocklin's ' House and Ocean' (Villa am Meer), I am at a loss. Did the handsome building appeal to me or the realistic medley of colours representing the ocean? I really couldn't say. I just knew, in some inexplicable way, that I was moved beyond words. That at one single moment, I was experiencing undiagnosed aches, unexplained pleasures. As we moved out of the Städel, we realized we had lost track of time and were late for an appointment with the Indian consul- general at India House. A marathon race past busy streets and the imposing fair tower - and we reached the place on time, out of breath. Ashok Kumar, the consul- general was most courteous and allowed us to wash off our tiredness with a cup of very Indian tea. He gave valuable tips on sightseeing in Frankfurt and after an interesting conversation on different issues, we took our leave.

 I was reminded of my meeting with Othmar Hardegger, consul at the Swiss general consulate. Maike Zeidler had invited me to a reading at the Literature House and saw to it that I mingled with the guests during the party later. I did smile at most of the faces I didn't know, and then found a cosy corner for myself. But trust Maike to pull me out of it into the crowd of guests! She introduced me to Othmar Hardegger, who hailed from that evergreen, beautiful land, Switzerland. He remembered his visit to India primarily as colours... and the colours were so strong that they still remained woven in his memories.

 Frankfurt had been nice to me...nice places, people, weather...the stuff that paintings are made of. What an experience – unexpected encounters, little grass flowers on the banks of the Main, quiet conversations, dreaming landscapes, clouds flirting with the earth.....a miracle immortalized in the paintings in the Städel.

As Walt Whitman would say:
Why, who makes much of a miracle?
As to me, I know nothing else but miracles.
Whether I walk the streets of Manhattan
Or talk by day with anyone I love
or sit at table at dinner with the rest.
To me, every hour of the light and dark is a miracle
What stranger miracles are there....!

A ticket to Berlin

The rise and fall of the Berlin Wall had always intrigued me. I remember the news clippings of November 9th 1989 when East Germany was collapsing before my eyes, there in my living – room in Odisha. Part of

the Iron Curtain, an iconic symbol of the Cold War, the Berlin Wall, was being torn down. Ever since, I had had a desire to visit Berlin. My husband was with me for a week and we decided to visit his friends in Berlin. Dr. Shreemanta Parida was a senior scientist at the Max Planck Institute for Infection Biology in Berlin, and Dr. Mayuri, his most enterprising wife. They had very patiently explained to us the various ticket options available for international travellers at the Hauptbahnhof, the central station.

Zipping across the German countryside on a pristine, high – speed inter – city express, quaint, story – book villages and church-bell chimes, well – manicured gardens and vast tracts of agricultural land, what more could one ask? In less than four hours we were moving into the Berlin Hauptbahnhof from Frankfurt, bright-eyed and ready to explore. Berlin, a re-modelled capital city that is both modern and classical, with a re-constituted Reichstag; the re-created beauty of Berlin beckoned. We crossed the Max Planck Institute, a historical edifice covered with a tapestry of startling green ivy. Our friends stay in the Mitte (central) area, the former East Berlin district now restored with luxury hotels and shopping arcades. Maike Zeidler had briefed us about the 'must see' spots and we did not want to lose a single minute.

Our first breath-taking moment was at the Brandenburg Tor, the gate designed by Carl Gotthard Langhans, modelled after the propylaeum of the Acropolis of Athens, situated in no - man's land between East and West Germany during the cold war and a symbol of the city's division as well as unification. We moved north of the gate towards the Reichstag, the building that had been the seat of the Weimar Republic and now housed the German Parliament. We climbed up the glass dome to have a magnificent view of Berlin, spread out carelessly on a carpet of history.

On to "Unter den Linden", the best street for a leisurely stroll, dotted with historic sites. We visited the Humboldt University at the Berlin Staatsoper, with its imposing pillars. The strains of a melodious organ wafted up to us from the St. Hedwigs – Kathedrale. Berlin, Alexanderplatz, named after the Russian Czar Alexander I and the massive Fernsehturm (TV tower). Postdamer Platz was used as a commercial and military transport centre before World War I. Among the large tracts of green belt we saw everywhere in Berlin was the Tiergarten (Zoo), laced with mysterious, meandering walkways. The Siegessäule (Victory Column) with a shining gold goddess of victory perched atop it stood in the centre of the park. We reached Check-Point Charlie and were soon engrossed in the fascinating accounts of the operation of the American Check-Point Charlie, the many escape attempts-both the tragic failures ending in death or the triumphant freedom gained by some. During the Cold War, this was one of the gates of the Berlin wall located in the centre of the city. As I stood there I wondered about the fragility of freedom....and Abraham Lincoln's words: 'Freedom is the last, best hope on Earth'.

It was raining as we reached Friedrichstraße, one of Berlin's largest and most elegant commercial districts. Soaked garments and umbrellas, deprecating glances, tired mouths. However, business proceeded as usual with indifference to the absolutely drenched mind I had. I was overwhelmed with the glimpses of history I had had. Despite being in the grip of change in the modern world, history matters. A story about the past, significant and true whispered to me by the ancient monuments and relics.

A short walk took us to the Holocaust Memorial

and my mind flew to a book which had made me cry in its painful depiction of tragedy, 'The Diary of Anne Frank'-an account of the atrocities of the Third Reich through the eyes of a young girl. Anne's diary was an oasis of hope in an unfair world. Her life, till her last breath in a concentration camp, was a celebration of optimism. Body and soul create a thousand possibilities and carve out many I's. But there is only one I in which there is a congruence of the creator and created, the I which Anne had stumbled upon. 'My sun sets to rise again', Robert Browning's immortal words were Anne's thoughts even in her last hours.

A long night. The road stretched limitlessly but Anne had overcome her fears – of the others, of herself, of death.

I had an appointment at the Berlin Literature House and we hurried to the Kurfürstendamm. We stopped before a sprawling villa, with a garden filled with a riot of colours. Like Frankfurt, the Berlin Literature House was a venue for readings, exhibitions and parties at the nearby restaurant. Mr. Ernest Wichner, the head of the house, was most cordial and showed me the whole place. It was an old building and appeared very cosy.

The Call of Leipzig

I was invited to visit Leipzig on the last leg of my trip to Germany. In the super-fast Inter-City Express, past picturesque villages, castles and white windmills on green pastures, we moved forward to Leipzig. A sun-streaked afternoon greeted us. Maike, my dear friend, had accompanied me to Leipzig. If I had thought Frankfurt was compact, then Leipzig was even more cosy. The Hauptbahnhof, the main train-station, an imposing building, was dotted with dazzling boutiques and shops. The city centre was snugly small and I saw a number of monuments as I strolled around -The old Town Hall, right in the middle of modern supermarkets and stores. The Nikolaikirche, audible from my room. Yes, the voice of the church, the tolling of the church bells came with the breeze right into my room. The opera house, theatre, the Bach house, the Thomaskirche, and many more. I had read about the University of Leipzig and many Germans of high repute who had studied there.

I also discovered that people here had discarded the much-debated theory of the famous evasive eye-contact of Germans. They looked directly at me and smiled and that instantly made me feel welcome in the state of Saxony. The languorous old - world charm, juxtaposed with classical, communist and modern buildings gave Leipzig an identity of its own. Of course, most of the buildings damaged in the Second World War had been restored, renovated. Dinner at the Alte Nikolaischule was steeped in history. I felt overwhelmed when I learnt that Wagner, whose compositions had given me so much pleasure, went to school here, all those years ago.

Leipzig had a long tradition of music and art. As a boy, Bach was in the Thomanerchor, St. Thomas Boys' Choir, which he directed and composed for until his death. Churches in town still perform his music, and the Bach museum is here. Johann Sebastian Bach, who went to India and even visited my home through his immortal compositions, had lived here. Some of his unforgettable pieces gave me immense pleasure, almost bordering on an exquisite pain. To imagine that all these great people had walked these streets, had had happy and sad moments and then left forever, as we all will do. But their footprints on "the sands of time," as Longfellow had written, are there for posterity.

My Leipzig trip had taken shape through the efforts of Birgit and Hannah at the Literature House. Birgit - always so poised - had been planning my sightseeing, and she informed me about Ralf Pannowitsch.

Seeing Leipzig with Ralf was an entirely novel experience. He seemed to know everything about everything and had a unique way of lacing his knowledge with modesty. We visited the Museum of Fine Arts, Christopher Schlingensief's strange Animatograph to Klinger's sketch, "New Dreams of Happiness". The intricate designs of Baroque style adorning Romano's house, a house which could never be a home for him, a house befitting a mayor, but not an unscrupulous one; Houses and their structures, styles all amazed me. He led me into covered passages with beautiful artwork on the ceilings, past gay flower shops. Oh yes! The doors that always open. In my hometown, you have to undergo scrutiny before the door is opened to a stranger. There are big signboards of "Beware of Dogs" hanging from gates, whether there is a dog or not. I was amazed how the doors were so friendly to a stranger, or was it because Ralf knew some secret code to open them?

And then, of course the lions, the cultural sentries of Leipzig, far from the forests, on rooftops, windows, above doors. Angry lions, happy ones, grave lions, handsome ones, almost like the many moods of Leipzig. I felt the lions' eyes on me, that famous eye-contact again! I knew that under the watchful eyes of the lions I would never get lost. After all the walking, we had a heavy lunch at "Coffee Baum" and a wonderful dessert called "apple strudel". Long ago I had read fascinating story-books in which the children always had apple strudel. I do know Ralf had been kind and was matching his rather fast pace with mine, but I was unmistakably slow and Germans walked fast. But he promised me tranquillity and peace in Connewitz and I could not resist. It was distinctly quieter as we walked down the lanes there. Ralf had promised to take me to his garden. I thought it would be a little green patch in front or back of a house. But no! Many acres of gardens at one end of the town, bought by people wanting quiet moments and a riot of colors; such a nice way to go gardening, almost an outing. The first thing I noticed about "Ralf's corner" was its own style, not rows of manicured plants but a wild splash of colours. Finding my way amidst the crowd of plants I saw a curious tenderness in Ralf, the way he introduced me to his apple trees, grape-vines and tomato plants, the velvety feel of rabbits' ears. What a storehouse of creativity, in the lap of a commercial centre like Leipzig. As we returned, some long – forgotten lines come to my mind:

The great challenge for the garden designer is not to make the garden look natural, but to make the garden so that the people in it will feel natural.
- Lawrence Halprin

Love is so short, forgetting is so long.
Visiting the Goethe House in Frankfurt was an unforgettable experience, the house that was home to the legendary writer Johann Wolfgang von Goethe. As I entered the premises, I closed my eyes, almost feeling the presence of Goethe. The celebrated writer's hometown had changed dramatically since his childhood, though his impressions can be recreated in the narrow streets leading up to the house. I walked around the house, awe-struck by the rich interior decoration, reconstructed, they say, to near perfection. Goethe's family had been well-to-do and well connected. His father had travelled widely and

brought back Roman marbles, rare books and paintings. He bequeathed to Goethe a passion for reading and a burning longing for Italy. The neat little kitchen, library, the picture gallery, Goethe's amateur paintings and of course the puppet theatre, all of it evoked so many images. My brief brush with Leipzig was almost like Goethe's intense affair when he lived there. "Leipzig's the place for me! "It is quite a little Paris; people there acquire a certain easy finish'd air," Goethe's characterization of Leipzig in his version of Faust. It was in Leipzig that the young Goethe encountered the original legend of Faust. He later used it as the basis of his famous drama, in which he immortalised the wine cellar Auerbachs Keller.

Almost reminded me of my very first day in Leipzig, where Birgit advised me to walk down to the Bach House, knowing all about my interest in music. Maike and I wound our way from the Altes Rathaus (the old town hall), across to the Thomaskirche where Bach had composed many immortal pieces on to his house, the house that was home to Johann Sebastian Bach. The lady in charge said they were closed for the day but eyeing my Indian attire and with Make's excellent negotiation skills, she allowed us a quick tour. Despite his famous choral, vocal and organ music, Bach was never accorded due recognition during his lifetime. I had seen the scars still left from the bombing attacks in World War II in some corners of Leipzig. But I know Bach's music survived all these nightmares and lives on in the smell and feel of Leipzig.

Ever since my arrival in Frankfurt, I had confided in Maike about my desire to go to the opera. The opera "Aida" is based on a story written by Egyptologist August Mariette, inspired by pharaonic history at its height. The story is about a victorious Egyptian pharaonic officer, Radamis. He falls in love with his captive Aida who tempts him to reveal to her his secret military plans. Pharaoh Ramses finds out about their secret and sentences Radamis to be walled up alive in a cellar till death. Aida herself hides in the cellar to face death with her lover. From the glittering lights of the opera house to the fabulous music, the fire and passion of the singers, the perfectly synchronized violin players, the well trained chorus, everything was a novel experience for me. The building itself was an architectural marvel. Though the singing style was very different from Indian classical in which I have been trained, it sounded good to my ears. Of course I know, the musical experience in a concert hall has a lot to do with good seating position and Maike had got me a good seat.

On the inaugural day of the Frankfurt book fair, I had briefly met Verena Nolte. After corresponding with her for over eight months regarding the project, I finally met her under a grumpy October sky, through a sheet of obstinate drizzle, right in front of the Messe Tower. And through the cold I found her exactly as I had imagined. warm, confident and friendly. Fatema, with a friendly streak in her, and as tall as Verena, had also come from Munich and with my fellow-writers, we made a cosy team. I feel privileged that I am a part of the world's largest trade fair for books, the Frankfurt Book Fair. I had never seen anything so huge, yet so systematic. There were bookstalls from all over the world with publishers, writers, academicians, translators, etc., networking and negotiating. I had a reading at the Arte stall along with the German writer, Angela Krauss. What was more exciting and a very pleasant co-incidence was that my mother, eminent Odia writer Pratibha Ray, was also a member of the Indian writers' delegation and although far from home, we had been brought together by the Frankfurt Book Fair. She marvelled at my familiarity with everything German, from streets, to historic sites, food, shops and ofcourse books. Frankfurter Buchmesse, where India was the Guest of Honour, along with literature drawn from most of its linguistic areas, was also an extended program of dance, art, music and film. I had the great opportunity of seeing Nobel laureates Gunter Grass, Imre Kertesz, and many other well-known literary figures.

One of my most cherished memories was representing India at the Frankfurt Book Fair as a recipient of the Goethe-German Literaturhaus fellowship for Creative and Travel writing. The world's biggest book fair opened its doors

in the German city of Frankfurt, with the guest of honour as India. I was privileged to share the stage with eminent German writer Angela Krauss. A freelance writer, she held the poetics lectureship at the University of Paderborn and was visiting theological faculty of the Humboldt University in Berlin.

We engaged in a dialogue, read from our works and spoke about the cultural diversity of our countries in literature. Later, during my visit to Leipzig, we both again came together for an evening of readings at the Leipzig Literaturhaus.

All good things come to an end; in this case, a very hurried end. Suddenly we were having our last dinner together. Strangely, despite the tug of home, there was a sadness at arriving at the full-stop. We were all together, Verena, Maike, Fatema, Martina, other representatives of the Goethe House and my fellow writers from India at an Italian restaurant where the food was very good, and we were all in high spirits, talking and laughing too much.

Maike had taken the trouble to teach me German songs in which I was extremely interested. She had a sweet voice and was a very encouraging teacher and I enjoyed my music lessons. Back home, I know I will present them in a concert. All the people I had met during my trip, all my friends, can they be forgotten? The old German lady at Zeil who had admired my scarf, the Blumen shop proprietress beneath my apartment, all those nice people at Literature House would all be far away soon.

As Neruda had written…
    'Love is so short, forgetting is so long….'.
    "It is the hour of departure, the hard cold hour
    which the night fastens to all the timetables.
    It is the hour of departure……."

Good-bye, Frankfurt!

The time had come, the hour of departure. I had to pack swiftly as Maike would be arriving any minute to drop me off at the airport. Were my suitcases really heavier or did they just seem so? So many things to pack, all tucked into the deep recesses of my memory. I looked around the apartment one last time, across the glass windows to the towers of Frankfurt, my guardian angels at night. I remembered the first tree I saw, the first raindrop, the first whiff of breeze across the Main. I knew that a seductive, sepia-colored nostalgia would go back with me and stay forever. I would retrace my steps down this month-long sojourn in Germany many times. When I would reminisce, I would probably remember everything, each place I saw, each monument, each relationship, communicating with fruit and flower, wind and rainbow.

But maybe with time, I would forget few things, life is like that; and as I would oscillate between remembrance and forgetting, I would relive the kaleidoscope of experiences.

Au revoir, Frankfurt!

FREIBURG

Sitting dainty at the edge of the Black Forest's wooded slopes and vineyards, Freiburg is a sunny, cheerful university town, its medieval tableau of gabled townhouses, cobblestone lanes and cafe-rimmed plazas. Blessed with unending hours of annual sunshine, it is Germany's warmest city. While neighbouring hilltop villages are still shovelling snow, the trees in Freiburg are clouds of white blossom, and locals are already enjoying in canal-side beer gardens. This eco-trailblazer has shrewdly tapped into that natural energy to generate nearly as much solar power as the whole of Britain, making it one of the country's greenest cities. With many architectural landmarks located within 15-20 minutes walking distance from one another (using Münster cathedral as the central focal point), we enjoyed walking along the cobblestone sidewalks while noticing many locals out on their bikes using the dedicated bicycle lane.

The Freiburg Bächle fascinated us – they are small water-filled tunnels that can be found throughout the old town. These were once common sights in many European cities during the Middle Ages, but only a few are left and Freiburg has one of the most complete systems in the world. They were originally used to fight fires, provide water and to cool off the city in those famously warm summers. Today of course, they are just for show, a pretty reminder of the past and a feature that locals and tourists alike have come to love. Surrounding the massive Freiburg Minster, the city's cathedral, is a daily market that has probably been in use for centuries. In the middle of town, it is the perfect location, and is a continuation of that important tradition, selling fruits and vegetables, flowers, toys and crafts and the famous cuckoo clocks. Adjacent to the Black Forest, Black Forest cake is naturally popular as are bakeries in general; I saw more in Freiburg than in any other German city I visited. More than just food, the active university life brings with it a number of shows and performances year-round, meaning a well-rounded cultural experience for tourists as well. It's just a really fun place to be, for all the right reasons.

BLACK FOREST

The Black Forest located in south west Germany is best known as being the place where many of the Grimm fairy-tales were based, an area immersed in folklore, fairy-tale and magic. It is a place of incredible beauty, spectacular waterfalls, age-old lakes, dense forests and mountains. The biggest town in the region is Freiburg, which is home to an ancient old town of pastel buildings.

The Black Forest is also as an unlikely foodie capital of the world. It is renowned for its spas and the cuckoo clocks produced in the region since the 1700s. The first thing that came to my mind when I heard about Black Forest was dark

chocolate cake with layers of cream, drenched in Kirsch with a cherry on top. Locally known as the Schwarzwald, the region got its name because its forests are so thick the locals called them black. Queen Victoria spent her holidays here, Victor Hugo visited often, and Mark Twain made it popular among Americans in one of his books by stating:

"Here you lose track of time in ten minutes and the world in twenty," Mark Twain in "A Tramp Abroad".

The vast forest stretches for a hundred miles along Germany's south-western borders. Its hills, valleys and forests stretch from the spa town of Baden-Baden to the Swiss border. As deep, dark and delicious as its famous cherry gateau, the Black Forest gets its name from its canopy of evergreens. With deeply carved valleys, thick woodlands, luscious meadows, strong timber farmhouses and sparkling waterfalls, it looks freshly painted for a kids' bedtime story. Wandering on its many miles of forest trails, we half expected to bump into a wicked witch or huntsman. I recollect with fondness the slow bus rides through the Black Forest.

A date with Mozart

SALZBURG

'Salzburg is storybook Austria. Standing beside the fast-flowing Salzach River, your gaze is raised inch by inch to the Altstadt's mosaic of graceful domes and spires, the formidable cliff-top fortress and the mountains beyond.'
–Lonely Planet

Just along the Bavarian border of Germany lies a neighbouring Austrian village that is straight out of a storybook. Salzburg is most commonly known as the birthplace of Mozart, or as the filming location for The Sound of Music, but this charming city is comprised of much more than just that. It's architecture boasts stunning medieval and baroque edifices, well-manicured parks are plentiful and a formidable cliff-top fortress set against the northern border of the Alps makes for breath-taking scenery. Yes, Salzburg is an idyllic combination of man-made and natural beauty.

Visiting Salzburg had been a fond dream come true experience. Ever since I had seen the movie "Sound of Music", I had been in love with Salzburg. It is an Austrian city on the border of Germany, with views of the Eastern Alps. The city is divided by the Salzach River, with medieval and baroque buildings of the pedestrian Altstadt (Old City) on its left bank, facing the 19th-century Neustadt (New City) on its right. The Altstadt, birthplace of famed composer Mozart is preserved as a museum displaying his childhood instruments.

Festung Hohensalzburg, Salzburg's landmark, is Central Europe's largest intact fortress and offers fantastic views of the city. The nearby vast Salzburg Dom is the main attraction of the old town. Mozart's Geburtshaus, the place where the master composer was born on January 27, 1756, is located in Getreidegasse, Salzburg's most attractive and visited shopping street with its high and narrow houses and romantic courtyards. Another highlight is Schloss Mirabell with its splendid gardens built by the Baroque master builder Lukas von Hildebrandt. Pegasus Statue Fountain, (the backdrop for "Do Re Mi"), Festival Hall complex (Edelweiss & So long, farewell) Residenz Square & Fountain (I have confidence in me) River Wolfgang, Mondsee, The cemetery, Nonnberg Abbey and so much more!! Salzburg is a mountain town with a gurgling river running right through the centre, music wafting in the air and a massive spread of rainbow touching just about everything!

Since times immemorial, the urge to travel has been spurred by a need. Be it the physician's advice for a change of place or a stress alleviation journey, a pilgrimage to places of religious importance or sight-seeing, music has now been interwoven to several tourism campaigns. Music tourism the world over takes a number of forms; as with any other kind of tourism, the commercial end manifests as the kind of mass commodification one sees in Vienna's Mozart chocolate wrappers or Elvis teddy-bears at Graceland. The other end is the complex set of attractions that draws visitors to particular places in order to listen to the music itself- Salzburg's sing-along Sound of music shows, or Gwalior's music sammelans celebrating the special aspects of the famous Tansen gharana or Bhubaneswar's grand music festivals.

Music Tourism grew significantly towards the end of the 20th century, and all forms of music, classical or folk, places of musical composition, places shown on celluloid that became associated with music (as the countryside shown in The Sound of Music) became favourite destinations. The famous "Sound of Music" tours in Salzburg function as a performative space for the construction and narration of Austrian national identity. or those related to a composers place of birth or his death became tourist attractions. Mozart, Bach, Strauss and other classical musicians were crowd pullers and Salzburg became a sort of stage to which tourists flocked. Equally popular was the Vienna Philharmonic Orchestra which played to packed audiences in two big halls, Musikverein and Konzerthaus.

HALLSTATT

Beautiful Hallstatt in Austria, one of the most serene towns, literally nestles in the lap of nature. It was our chosen offbeat destination in our trip to Salzburg. A picture perfect town with amazing views, we had chosen to drive with a desire to discover these dreamy, anonymous towns. Bright red and yellow hues adorned the Austrian town's 16th-century architecture; it was summer in full bloom when I was visiting and the flower boxes draped the windows in geraniums and ivy. The cobblestone streets connecting to charming cafés, ornate churches, and Alpine inns made it a magical experience. There were natural wonders to be discovered around every corner—from the neighbouring Salzkammergut mountains to Lake Hallstatt to the village's very own waterfall.

    Hugged by a tranquil lake on one side and the imposing mountains on the other, it made my heart stop with its serene grace. We spent long hours near the lake, with a terrific view of the historic Alpine houses Hallstatt is famous for. The nature trails were the very best, offering an anonymity rare to find in the well-known tourist spots. It is a town steeped in history and the local community has kept the authenticity intact. More than 7000 years old, it is home to the oldest salt mine in the world and so is listed among the UNESCO sites.

VIENNA

'Vienna wasn't just a city, it was a tone that either one carries forever in one's soul or one does not. It was the most beautiful thing in my life.'

Sanders Marai, Embers

If a picture can paint a thousand words, then I have a million after my Vienna visit. Vienna, a place steeped in history, music, and exotic tales of princesses and kings. It is real and it is all in Vienna, Austria. Additional to being known as the "City of Music" due to its musical legacy, Vienna is also said to be the "City of Dreams", because of it being home to the world's first psychoanalyst, Sigmund Freud. Vienna's ancestral roots lie in early Celtic and Roman settlements that transformed into a Medieval and Baroque city. Austria's Imperial capital offers a unique blend of imperial traditions and stunning modern architecture. It is famous for its cultural events, imperial sights, coffee houses, cozy wine taverns, and the very special Viennese charm.

There was an unmistakable feeling of royalty we got at the magnificent Schönbrunn Palace which can probably best be compared to Paris' Versailles – or at least that's what the locals say. There's also the Hofburg Palace in the city centre. Vienna is an ideal destination for art lovers. At the Museums Quarter, there are several options to choose from and their close proximity to each other is convenient. The buildings are designed in a combination of baroque and contemporary architectural styles and the outdoor space becomes a meeting spot for locals throughout the day and especially in the summertime. There are comfortable chairs and several bars and restaurants around the square if you need a break between museum hopping. Another major attraction is Belvedere, a complex consisting of two Baroque palaces, an Orangery and the Palace Stables. My main motivation for visiting Belvedere was to marvel upon Klimt's 'The Kiss'. Something about the colors and the intensity of the lovers' embrace captivated my emotions so much that I could not move from that spot for a good twenty minutes.

Vienna owes much of its international fame to the many celebrated composers who lived and worked here including Strauß, Mozart, Beethoven and Haydn. The Vienna Philharmonic Orchestra is one of the world's best, the Staatsoper one of the world's leading opera houses, and the Vienna Boys' Choir, one the world's most famous. Vienna has established itself as a great musical metropolis.

In Vienna, traditional coffee houses, rustic wine taverns, and the beloved sausage stand (Wuerstelstand) exist alongside top restaurants and shops. Time-honoured events alternate with internationally-acclaimed extravaganzas (Life Ball) to create a unique and very special ambiance. Another special feature of Vienna is its many green spaces and recreational areas such as the Wienerwald, the Prater, and the Donauinsel.

Sigmund Freud's home

"It is dark in me. My consciousness is a lonely light."

Reading the books written by "Freud" had always made me ponder on the unfathomable mysteries of the mind and the shadowy origins of psychoanalysis. I was fortunate to have visited Freud's house on the Bergasse in Vienna. As I wandered through the rooms where he had lived once, I felt somewhat surreal, lighter than air yet oddly connected to the ground. I continue to remain enthralled by the elusive mystery that sometimes emerges from the vast deep planes of the individual and collective unconscious, expressed through the body and through speech and shared between therapist, client and who knows what else in the far beyond.

Mozarthaus

W. A. Mozart: *"I confess all these, my sins, in the hope that I may be permitted to confess them more often."*

Wolfgang Amadeus Mozart, baptised as Johannes Chrysostomus Wolfgangus Theophilus Mozart, was a prolific and influential composer of the Classical period. Born in Salzburg, Mozart showed prodigious ability from his earliest childhood. I have had a fascination with Mozart ever since I was introduced to his symphonies. Why Mozart? Because he had quality contributions work in every genre: symphonies, concertos for strings and other instruments,

choral music, songs, serious operas, comic operas, chamber music, solo sonatas, sacred music and so on.

Though Mozart lived at different addresses in Vienna, the only apartment that has survived to this day is at Domgasse number 5. The composer lived at this address from 1784 till 1787.Wolfgang Amadeus spent the happiest years of his life here. Particularly during this period, Mozart was a celebrated composer, had an illustrious circle of friends, and was asked to give countless concerts at the houses of the nobility. It was here at Domgasse that he also penned his best compositions, including what is perhaps his most popular opera The Marriage of Figaro. Occupying 1,000 square meters on six levels, the Mozarthaus was opened on January 27, 2006 – the 250th anniversary of Mozart's birth.

The romance of Prague

PRAGUE-PRAHA

The name actually meant "threshold". The city was a portal between the life of the good and the other. A city of dark magic. The wind carried the memory of magic, revolution, violins, and the cobbled lanes meandered like creeks. Some wore Mozart wigs and pushed chamber music on street corners, and marionettes hung in windows, making the whole city seem like a theatre with unseen puppeteers crouched behind velvet."

Walking through a local market selling knickknacks of all sort, from hand carved marionettes and puppets, a popular Czech craft dating back to the 18th century was

an authentic experience. The Charles Bridge connects the city's Old Town to Prague Castle and is adorned with 30 baroque-style statues. The statue of John of Nepomuk is notably famous for its plaque featuring the falling priest. Stopping to rub the plaque is supposed to bring good luck and ensure your return to Prague. Of course we did it! Who would not wish to return to this magical destination?

What made Prague more special to me was that it had been home to famous writers Franz Kafka, Milan Kundera, poet Rainer Maria Rilke, immortal composer Mozart to name a few. The cultural history of Prague is intimately intertwined with these writers. Beautiful Prague has also been a victim of "over-tourism". A phenomenon more commonly associated with destinations such as Barcelona, Amsterdam, Venice and Edinburgh, has arrived in Prague – a city that was all but sealed off to western visitors until 1989 when the velvet revolution swept the former communist regime from power.

Walking around Prague is comparable to being in a fairy tale, except for one minor detail: it's real. Prague, the golden city of a thousand spires, is at the epicentre of Bohemia and has emerged from its years behind the Iron Curtain as an international centre for poetry and the arts. The city is amazingly well preserved (despite the bombing of World War II). Despite the brief time we had at Prague, we had our fill of the quaint old town with its cobbled paths, Gothic and Baroque architecture.

Walking with history at Quebec

QUEBEC CITY

Québec City nestles on the banks of the Saint Lawrence River in Canada's predominantly French-speaking Québec province. it has a fortified colonial core, Vieux-Québec and Place Royale, with stone buildings and quaint, narrow streets. This area is the site of the towering Château Frontenac Hotel and imposing Citadelle of Québec. The Petit Champlain district's cobblestone streets are lined with bistros and boutiques that are a tourist's delight.

We were at Quebec with my brother's family, Ayaskant, Ashita and Akshara, and that added so much more fun to the whole experience. Despite a light drizzle, we walked the streets to the Fairmont Le Château Frontenac which is the iconic centre-piece of the UNESCO World Heritage neighbourhood of Old Québec. The hotel is known for its high-profile guests who range from Charles Lindbergh to Celine Dion. Lunch at a sidewalk cafe, trudging aimlessly on unknown cobblestone lanes, and enjoying the French language filling the streets, we almost thought we were in Paris. Québec City holds an unmistakable European charm. The breath-taking architecture of the Cathedral-Basilica of Notre-Dame de Québec, street performers filling the air with music, tasting local cuisine and simply, taking in the beauty all around, all made it a lifetime's experience.

The Historic District of Old Quebec is one of the UNESCO World Heritage Sites in Canada. It is considered a world heritage treasure. Every corner of this historic district is teeming with history. Hence, it is also one of the most popular tourist destinations in Canada.

We had also visited the Rideau Canal, a UNESCO World heritage centre also known as the Rideau Waterway.

It connects the city of Ottawa, Ontarioon the Ottawa River to the city of Kingston, Ontario, on Lake Ontario and is 202 kilometres in length. Apart from the sightseeing highlights of Ottawa, we loved the walk trail along the Canal. I spent memorable days at breath-taking Niagara Falls. Watching it from both Canada and US had been equally amazing. Few natural wonders have inspired the imagination of so many as Niagara, from poets and politicians to ordinary sightseers and tourists. From majestic Niagara to Sound-of- Music style impromptu picnics, Horn-blowers Cruise and exploring Lundy's lane and Clifton Hill, it was a great adventure till the finish. The list would be incomplete without mention of our visit to Chippawa historic village, on the shores of Niagara river.The village was founded in 1850, and became part of the City of Niagara Falls, Ontario by amalgamation. In historic documents, the name of the village and the river is also spelled as Chippewa or Chippeway. As it happens when tourists search for destinations far from the madding crowd, the Chippawa area is a popular niche tourism spot. Home to golf courses, parks, the historic field of the Battle of Chippawa, attractive architecture and a quiet atmosphere, it attracts crowds. Marineland is also located just outside the village. The village is dotted with several small eateries, antiques shops, Chippawa House and Chippawa Town Hall. Quebec, however, remained our favourite!

Italy

Olive groves, gelato and a Roman Holiday

ROME

"Rome is not like any other city. It's a big museum, a living room that shall be crossed on one's toes." – Alberto Sordi

Ever since I had watched the endearing romantic musical "Roman Holiday", I had yearned to visit Rome. Rome, one of Europe's oldest cities was founded in 753. BC. by Romulus and Remus. Rome is one of the most iconic and most travelled to cities in Europe, with a mixture of cultures from around the world. Wandering around the cobblestone streets with gelato in hand, spending time watching tourists from the Spanish Steps and taking in all of the stunning architecture the city had to offer, I did it all. We opted for wandering around by foot— the most romantic way to discover the hidden corners of the city— but we did use the impressive public system of buses and trolleys.

The neighbourhoods of Centro Storico (the historical centre of Rome) and Ancient Rome are the heart of the city where most of Rome's iconic sights are located. This area

is also tourist central and we had to deal with the crowds, street performers, souvenir shops, and outrageously expensive restaurants. Notwithstanding, it's still one of the most beautiful places on Earth. The "modern" centre of Rome is a mix old and new. It is also home to most of Rome's hotels, dining, and nightlife.

Bede wrote in 7th century AD, "As long as the Colosseum stands, Rome shall stand; when the Colosseum falls, Rome shall fall; and when Rome falls, the world will end."

Also known as the Flavian Amphitheatre, it is an oval amphitheatre in the centre of the city of Rome, Italy. Built of travertine, tuff, and brick-faced concrete, it is the largest amphitheatre ever built. The Colosseum is situated east of the Roman Forum. Being able to sit close to 50,000 spectators, it was the premier venue for wild beast shows and bloody gladiator combat. During the inauguration games (that lasted 100 days and nights) about 5000 wild animals were slaughtered. Rhinos, crocodiles, bears, elephants, lions, tigers and giraffes were victims of the animal hunt shows that took place in the Colosseum.

The Trevi Fountain, in the Quirinale district in Rome, is a popular destination for tourists to visit. Known as one of the most beautiful fountains in the world, it was made even more famous by some of the movies that it is featured in, such as La Dolce Vita, where Anita Ekberg frolics through the water fully clothed. It was designed by Italian architect Nicola Salvi and completed by Giuseppe Pannini. Standing a little more than 25 metres high and around 50 meters wide, it is the largest Baroque fountain in the city and one of the most famous fountains in the world. I did throw my wish coin in the fountain, with my friend Mary, to return to romantic Rome again!

Vatican City, a city-state surrounded by Rome, Italy, is the headquarters of the Roman Catholic Church. It's home to the Pope and a trove of iconic art and architecture. Its Vatican Museums house ancient Roman sculptures such as the famed "Laocoön and His Sons" as well as Renaissance frescoes in the Raphael Rooms and the Sistine Chapel, famous for Michelangelo's ceiling. Rome has more spectacular museums, churches, squares, fountains, and ancient ruins per square foot than just about anywhere else in the world. Everywhere we went, you'll see something amazing.

PALERMO, SICILY

I was selected to be part of a global think-tank on "Global Tourism Trends: What's on the horizon for tourists and travellers?" on the occasion of the Indian Tourism and Hospitality Congress & University School Of Tourism (ScuolaUniversitariaEuropea per ilTurismo) Italy 11th International Tourism Conference on "Innovations and Opportunities in Global Tourism" The Inaugural session of the International Congress of Tourism organized by UET(Milan, Rome and Palermo) & Pegaso Universita Telematica

was at the majestic Palazzo Mazzarino, with luminaries of the tourism fraternity of Sicily, delegates and students. My amazement at the wonderful architecture and structures made me agree with what travellers describe it as – Italy's best-kept secret.

"I was enchanted… the limpidity of the sky, the restless splendour of the sun, the beauty of the countryside, a certain excitement of the fantasy…which brought to mind the time when in the fields one encountered the divine."

(John Houel, 1735 – 1813 French painter on Sicily)

The Sicilian capital, called the "Kingdom of the Sun" by invading Normans in the 12th century, has been a cultural melting pot since Phoenicians and Greeks fought over it in the 5th and 6th centuries BC. Sitting close to where Europe ends and Africa begins, Palermo bears the scar marks – yet reflects the glories – of centuries of domination. Once Roman, Byzantine, Arab, Norman and ultimately Italian, it has a relatively recent "made in Italy" identity. It has basked under the banner of being the Italian Capital of Culture.

Palermo is the capital of the Italian island of Sicily. The 12th-century Palermo Cathedral houses royal tombs, while the huge neoclassical Teatro Massimo is known for opera performances. Also in the center are the Palazzo dei Normanni, a royal palace started in the 9th century, and the Cappella Palatina, with Byzantine mosaics. Busy markets include the central Ballarò street market and the Vucciria, near the port. A fascinating walking tour through the quaint streets of Palermo, steeped in culture! Baroque structures, stained glass paintings, way-side piano recitals & the warmth of Italians, a memorable experience indeed!

At the intersection of Via Maqueda and Corso

Vittorio Emanuele is Piazza Vigliena, whose four baroque corners mark the centre of the historic quarter, locally known as Quattro Canti. Immediately south and east is grandiose Piazza Pretoria, also known as Piazza della Vergogna, the square of shame, for the thoroughly naked statues of nymphs, tritons and leaping river gods (senza veli, without veils) adorning the magnificent circular fountain in front of the Palazzo Pretorio (City Hall). In the streets around are stunning 12th-century churches, Arab-Norman Chiesa Santa Maria dell' Ammiraglio, Chiesa Capitolare di San Cataldo with its distinct faded red domes, and the baroque 16th-century Chiesa di Santa Caterina.

The history of the Grand Hotel Villa Igiea where we had a special dinner– a masterpiece of Sicilian Art Nouveau – is linked to the encounter between two famous Palermo-born men: Ignazio Florio Jr and Ernesto Basile. The former was the heir of one of the most notable and rich families in Italy at the time: the Florios owned banks, factories, shipyards and countless activities. He was the man behind some of the historic enterprises on the island: building the Teatro Massimo (where Enrico Caruso would be "discovered") and establishing the "Ceramiche Florio" factory, the Consorzio Agrario Siciliano (Sicilian Agrarian Consortium), Palermo's shipyard, and the daily newspaper "L'Ora".

The latter instead created many of the splendid buildings in the Sicilian capital: casa Utveggio, villino Fassini ('villino' literally means "small villa"), villino Basile. And, first and foremost, villino Florio inside Olivuzza Park, Italy's first Art Nouveau building, which he was commissioned to build by Florio – who also entrusted him with designing the Teatro Massimo.

Thus, in the late 19th century, the fruitful relationship between these two men resulted in a beautiful building – decorated by Ettore De Maria Bergler and furnished in a wonderful floral style by Vittorio Ducrot – that today is considered one of the most luxurious hotels in the region.

CEFALU, SICILY

Anchored between salty water and craggy rock sits the charming small town of Cefalù. An ancient fishing port at heart, in relatively recent years it has become the beach-side break of choice for those seeking sun and sand along the Tyrrhenian coast of Sicily. Cefalù is a coastal city in northern Sicily, Italy.

In the cooler early morning hours, the warren-like tangle of streets are filled with people, but the obvious mix of locals alongside the well, not-so-local, is refreshing. Even the beach, this perfect crescent slither of biscuit coloured sand, heaving under the weight of a thousand colourful umbrellas screams out to all who pass to give in, lie down and simply live the dolce vita for a little while.

It's known for its Norman cathedral, a 12th-century fortress-like structure with elaborate Byzantine mosaics and soaring twin towers. Nearby, the Mandralisca Museum is home to archaeological exhibits and a picture gallery with a portrait by Antonello da Messina. The beaches of Mazzaforno and Settefrati lie to the west. After half a day's brainstorming at the conference, we set out for Cefalu. I was lucky to get a window seat in the bus and enjoyed the sublime views of the emerald green sea and small rocky coves immensely.

At both ends of the beach there were public bathing areas which were understandably much busier with beach goers bringing their own sunshades and windbreaks creating a traditional seaside picture. The clear, turquoise blue sea looked very inviting. Despite Cefalu being a tourist town it has managed to retain a tasteful, calm appearance and was just perfect for a gentle stroll. After some window shopping we arrived at Piazza Duomo from where we admired Cefalu's huge cathedral. A set of stone steps provided access to its main entrance and inside we marvelled at its mosaic adorned interior and large, marble pillars.

La Rocca or the "Rock" as it is referred to is a large rock formation which casts a shadow on the village and makes up a very scenic backdrop to the village. There are some ruins remaining at the top of the rock. There is a path that leads to the top of La Rocca and it passes the ruins of the Temple of Diana along the way. At the top is what is thought to be the ruins of a 13th-century castle known as the Cefalu Castle. With its great view of the coast and the village below, the castle was a key to protecting the town and its harbour.

Switzerland

The Call of the Swiss Alps

INTERLAKEN

Interlaken is a traditional resort town in the Bernese Oberland region of central Switzerland. Nestling on a narrow stretch of valley, between the emerald-tinted waters of Lake Thun and Lake Brienz, it has old timber houses and parklands on both sides of the Aare River. The surrounding mountains, with dense forests, alpine meadows and glaciers, has numerous hiking and skiing trails. Scenic sightseeing tours by train are very popular as this region which is home to Europe's highest railroads. We indulged in unique Swiss culinary experience, with cheese and chocolate sampling tours that began at Interlaken town, the old Interlaken Abbey, a 900-year-old Swiss heritage gem, or simply took long, rambling walks, soaking in the splendour of the surrounding peaks and tranquil lake waters. Interlaken, ofcourse is a popular destination for Bollywood movies.

BADEN

This is one of my precious travel memories. We were all together with my mother at Zurich, attending an international conference at the ETH Zürich, (Eidgenössische Technische Hochschule, Swiss Federal Institute of Technology) a public research university in the city of Zürich, Switzerland. But after the conference, we explored several destinations nearabouts and that is how we reached Baden that sunny morning. The town has been famous as a lively curative resort since Roman times, when Baden was known as "Aquae Helveticae". A bathing quarter with grand buildings, to help offer relief to victims of rheumatism and circulatory diseases, was an early town feature on the shores of the river Limmat. Notable people such as Goethe, Nietzsche and Dürrenmatt sought out the Baden thermal springs in which to relax.

    We strolled along the car-free old town with its historic structures and municipal buildings, theatres and museums being the other cultural attractions. The Langmatt Foundation is one of Switzerland's finest art collections – the industrialist families Brown and Boveri bequeathed valuable paintings and furniture dating from the impressionist period. We enjoyed the hiking trials, the local food and the swiss magic spread lavishly in the scenic beauty all around.

The Shakespeare Trail

STRATFORD-ON-AVON

My very first visit to Stratford-upon- Avon, William Shakespeare's hometown and we were super excited.

Stratford-upon-Avon, a medieval market town in England's West Midlands, is the 16th-century birthplace of Shakespeare, possibly the most famous writer in the English language, known for his sonnets and plays, 'Romeo and Juliet' and 'Hamlet' etc. The Royal Shakespeare Company performs his plays in the Royal Shakespeare Theatre and adjacent Swan Theatre on the banks of the River Avon.

We were eager to see everything, from Shakespeare's house to the Old Town. There were quaint cafes and restaurants, and many beautiful parks, gardens, and historic buildings to admire, too. The breath-taking views of the English countryside was a writer's delight. The town was decked with flowers and pathways leading to different places of interest. The birthplace of William Shakespeare was a timber thatched-white and chocolate coloured house not far from the river, Avon. There were some shops and lots of bakeries selling afternoon tea. The tour of Shakespeare's birthplace was an amazing experience. The guides were extremely knowledgeable recounted interesting stories about Shakespeare's life and family. We were spellbound to move around the house where Shakespeare had grown up. We then walked through town to Anne Hathaway's Cottage. This historic thatched-roof house was Shakespeare's wife's family home. When we had completed the Shakespeare circuit, we focussed the rest of our time in Stratford-upon-Avon on exploring the Old Town. The half-timbered facades and ye-olde-everything delight our eyes, and we just could not get enough of Sheep Street, Henley Street, and Church Street.

Loch Ness and Scottish Highlands

EDINBURGH

Edinburgh
The Unesco City of Literature

''To travel hopefully is a better thing than to arrive.''

Fascinating tapestries of history, the kaleidoscope of culture, gorgeous panoramic vistas, delicious food and drink – Edinburgh is one of those cities with a bit of just about everything The Scottish capital was abundantly charming, a unique amalgamation of its medieval Old Town and an elegant Georgian New Town. I found an unmistakable charm of this city filled with amazing gothic architecture. The Edinburgh Castle dating back to the 7th century was an unmistakable attraction. The Royal Mile is Edinburgh's oldest and most famous street, running from the castle at one end to the Palace of Holyrood house at the other. The Mile was busy and bustling and there was always something going on – from street theatre to fire-throwing bagpipers, regal churches, historic buildings, cafés and bars to explore, as well as all the food shops one could ever need!

Edinburgh has long been a haven for literature lovers, and provides a wide choice of cosy cafés for quiet moments with a good book. But I had loved wandering around and experiencing first-hand the quaint streets. My date with the writers: Robert Louis Stevenson, Sir Walter Scott, Robert Burns was at the Writer's Museum. Makars Court, hidden at the top of the Royal Mile, is a tranquil courtyard with carved paving stones celebrating writers from the 14th century to the present day. I had my fill of wonderful portraits, rare books and personal objects including Burns' writing desk, the printing press on which Walter Scott's Waverley novels were first produced, and items from Stevenson's travels around the world.

"This is a city of shifting light, of changing skies, of sudden vistas. A city so beautiful it breaks the heart again and again."

(Alexander McCall Smith)
Edinburgh, Scotland.

The Writers' Museum, in Lady Stair's House at the Lawnmarket, on the Royal Mile in Edinburgh, presents the lives of three of the foremost Scottish writers: Robert Burns, Walter Scott and Robert Louis Stevenson. It is an institution that conserves and exhibits rare books, manuscripts, portraits, and personal items belonging to the beloved 18th-century poet Burns; the 18th and 19th-century poet, novelist, and historian Scott; and 19th-century novelist Stevenson, famous for Treasure Island and The Strange Case of Dr. Jekyll and Mr. Hyde.

Among the highlights of the Writers' Museum are first editions of Stevenson's A Child's Garden of Verses and Scott's popular 19th-century novel entitled Waverley; the printing press that produced Waverly; Burns' writing desk; and one of the three plaster casts made of Burns' skull. I also saw Stevenson's riding boots; a ring gifted by a Samoan chief engraved with the word Tusitala, meaning "teller of tales;" his wardrobe, crafted by the notorious 18th-century Scottish cabinet maker Deacon Brodie, who is believed to have been the inspiration for The Strange Case of Dr. Jekyll and Mr. Hyde.

And how can I forget the university! The University of Edinburgh, founded in 1582, is one of Scotland's ancient universities. The university has five main campuses in the

city of Edinburgh, with many of the buildings in the historic Old Town belonging to the university.

"It's like everyone tells a story about themselves inside their own head. Always. All the time. That story makes you what you are. We build ourselves out of that story."

(Patrick Rothfuss), The Name of the Wind

Visiting The Scottish Storytelling Centre at Edinburgh was an unforgettable experience for me. A haven for Scotland's culture-lovers, it presents series of exciting programmes of literature, readings, storytelling, theatre and traditional arts, along with exhibitions and workshops. I spent an entire afternoon there and it was still not quite enough.

The Bagpiper at Edinburgh Castle:

No sound is more emblematic of Scotland than the bagpipes. It is said that this national instrument originally from Egypt, was first played here in the late 1500s. I had the wonderful experience of being serenaded by a flamboyant piper at the top of Calton Hill, with all the city spread out beneath us.

Bagpipes are a class of musical instrument, using enclosed reeds fed from a constant reservoir of air in the form of a bag. Though the Scottish Great Highland bagpipes have the greatest visibility in the English-speaking world, bagpipes have been played for centuries throughout large parts of Europe, Turkey, the Caucasus, around the Persian Gulf, Northern Africa and North America.

The high-point of our trip was certainly the breath-taking vistas of Scottish Highlands. Glencoe is a quaint village in western Scotland, tucked steep-sided into Glencoe valley, in the Scottish Highlands. Known for sparkling waterfalls and trails that lead to peaks such as Buachaille

Etive Mor and Bidean nam Bian. In the village, Glencoe is a huddle18th-century thatched cottages, a symbol of the local heritage. The highlands of Scotland are one of the most heavenly places I have visited. Famous for awe-inspiring mountains, rare wildlife, lush greenery, and tranquil lochs, it is a huge spread of a beautiful painting. Film-makers have extensively used Glencoe as a classic backdrop in many movies: for stupendous mountain scenery, towering peaks and intensely deep lochs and for vast stretches of empty space. We were excited to see some of the famous locales used in Skyfall. The Pass of Glencoe, with the shape of the Three Sisters, has been used a s a back-drop for *Highlander (1986)*, *Restless Natives (1985)*, *The 39 Steps (1935)*, *Made of Honor (2008)*, *Harry Potter and the Deathly Hallows (2010/11)*, *The Eagle (2011)* or *Rob Roy (1995)* etc.

The culmination of this trip was a visit to Loch-Ness, a destination I had craved to see ever since my school days, when I first heard about the mysterious monster. A large freshwater lake in the Scottish Highlands, Loch Ness is the second-largest and second-deepest lake in Scotland connecting to River Oich at its southern end. Home to the Loch Ness monster – a famous mythical creature believed to be living amidst the depths of the lake – it attracts a steady flow of tourists in all seasons. Alleged views of the Loch Ness monster, popularly known as Nessie by the locals, draws tourists from all over the world to this destination.

I must also write about the Scottish traditional delights I savoured during this trip. Scotland is home to varieties of food, from fresh sea-food and traditional haggis, to colourful vegan dishes and delicious locally sourced ingredients. I did enjoy all this and the spread of the typical Scottish breakfast, apart from my favourite fish n chips.

Canyon Roads and Vegas Lanes

GRAND CANYON NATIONAL PARK
ARIZONA
One of the seven natural wonders of the world
Unesco World heritage Centre

Grand Canyon National Park encompasses canyons, river tributaries, and surrounding grounds. The Grand Canyon is situated in Arizona's north-western quadrant. With millions of visitors making the trip to the canyon each year, this park is one of the most visited tourist destinations in the world. In addition, the park has been a UNESCO World Heritage Site since 1979. The Grand Canyon had a long and arduous road to becoming

a national park, beginning in the 1880's with several failed congressional bills. After making multiple visits to the area, Theodore Roosevelt declared the Grand Canyon a National Monument in 1908. Vast and strikingly beautiful, the Grand Canyon is Arizona's most famous landmark-and a natural wonder you must see to believe. Elongating 277 miles (446 kilometers) in length from end to end, steep, rocky walls descend more than a mile to the canyon's floor, where the wild Colorado River traces a swift course southwest.

We fell in love with Grand Canyon at first sight. As we walked deeper into the canyons within the Canyon, the immensity and wonder of it all was reminder of our smallness against the smallness vis-à-vis its vastness. On the rim there was this once in a lifetime, breathtaking view awaiting us– the sun and the air were endless silver tricks – the light of the sun with crimson stratagems – the changes were going on in split seconds – the azure blues slid down a box of yellow and mixed with reds that melted into gray and came back saffron clay and granite pink. It was not a particularly overcrowded day, but we walked several yards away from other tourists and found our own secluded spot where it was just us and a cinemascope view of the canyon.

We were fortunate to have got the opportunity to sit at the rim at sunset and watch the colours change in a kaleidoscope. Some of our best photos and memories were created in those moments.

BRYCE CANYON NATIONAL PARK
Garfield County and Kane County
UTAH

Bryce Canyon is not a single canyon, but a series of natural amphitheatres or bowls, carved into the edge of a high plateau. The most famous of these is the Bryce Amphitheatre, which is filled with irregularly eroded spires of rocks called hoodoos. Perhaps every visitor to the park, like us, intended to spend time marvelling at its four main viewpoints, all found within the first few miles of the park: Bryce Point, Inspiration Point, Sunset Point, and Sunrise Point.

A land of delicately carved rock spires, Bryce Canyon was an out-of-this-world start to our US national park hopping. The park is filled with thousands of rock formations called hoodoos. They are formed when the

Author with family at Bryce Canyon National Park

limestone is eroded by wind, frost and rain, shaping it into an assortment of canyons, fins, arches and spires. Iron oxide in the rock gives it a vivid red, orange or yellow's tint. According to the official website, "The erosional force of frost-wedging and the dissolving power of rainwater have shaped the colourful calcium-rich mud-stone into bizarre shapes, including slot canyons, windows, fins, and spires called 'hoodoos'."

The canyon gets its name from Ebenezer Bryce, a Mormon pioneer and shipbuilder who settled in the valley in 1870. He built roads and started off the settlement here, but was notoriously uneffusive about his spectacular home, describing it as "a hell of a place to lose a cow".

We explored Bryce Canyon by walking along a series of overlooks and trails along the top of the rim. It was a clear, sunny day and we could see over 150 miles because of the high altitude and clear air up there. We felt we were on the edge of another world.

LAS VEGAS

The City of Second Chances

When we reached Las Vegas we had a thirst for places, gardens and wilderness, almost everything about this dream destination. We got out to the streets and savoured the experience of wandering about in the open air to examine the architecture, the spectacles, and the stuff for sale, surprises and strangers. Belaggio Hotel and Casino, where we stayed was the ultimate experience in luxury. Bellagio's elaborately floral lobby, its blown-glass Dale Chihuly ceiling, remains one of the most fabulous sights in Las Vegas. It opens into the Conservatory and Botanical Gardens, inspired by verdigris-framed Parisian gardens,

Author with family at different destinations of Las Vegas

and is fronted by the iconic Bellagio Fountains, where people cluster every single evening to take in the city's best public show.

What happens in Vegas doesn't always stay in Vegas.... walking down the 'Strip', from Mandalay Bay down to Treasure Island...casino's, Bellagio Fountains, Venetian fun and late night sprees, Lalit's saxophone recitals on the strip...all we can say is 'encore'!

The temples of the Gods

CAIRO
EGYPT

The Great Sphinx of Giza
Nazlet El-Semman, Al Haram,
Giza Governorate, Cairo

I had dreamt about visiting The Pyramids of Giza ever since I had read about it in my 4th standard at school. The Great Sphinx of Giza is a sculpture of a lion sprawled out, with the head of an Egyptian king, carved out of limestone on the Giza plateau probably in the reign of King Khafre (2558-2532 BCE) during the period of the Old Kingdom of Egypt. Facing towards the rising sun, it is located on the Giza plateau, few kilometres west of Cairo, on the west bank of the Nile River. Egyptian rulers worshipped it as a symbol of the sun god, calling it Hor-Em-Akhet ("Horus of the Horizon"). The Sphinx sits in part on the necropolis of ancient Memphis, the seat of power for the

pharaohs, a short distance from three large pyramids – the Great Pyramid of Khufu (Cheops), Khafre (Chephren) and Menkaura (Mycerinus).

In Greek tradition, the sphinx has the head of a woman, the haunches of a lion, and the wings of a bird. She is mythically portrayed as treacherous and merciless. Those who cannot answer her riddle suffer a fate typical in such mythological stories, as they are killed and eaten by this ravenous monster. It was one of the most awesome experiences, standing in the sizzling heat and looking at this amazing wonder, at history spread all around. The overcrowded bazaars of Cairo could not deter us from our regular walks to the university and museums. The Museum of Egyptian Antiquities, also known as the Egyptian Museum or Cairo Museum, housed a huge collection of ancient Egyptian antiquities. The visit to Khan el-Khalili will remain etched in my mind for all times. It is a noisy and chaotic bazaar with Egyptians and tourists flocking the market for their routine as also for spice and jewellery. The lanes of Khan el-Khalili were lined with small shops dealing in souvenirs, antiques, jewellery and semi-precious stones and we picked gifts for our family back home.

The land of Nefertiti & Tutankhamen, of Pharaohs and mysterious hieroglyph on papyrus, Cleopatra's cosmetics and Egyptian perfumes, all put together, was an out of the world experience. My mother had been my travel companion for that trip. We had an unforgettable cruise on River Nile, accompanied by Sufi dancers and an Egyptian wedding troupe.

We were accompanied by a young Egyptologist as a guide and so got a vivid account of history made easy. After the fascinating encounter with Cairo, we visited yet another cultural seat of mystery, Luxor. Notwithstanding

Luxor's many sites worth seeing, the most famous is the Valley of the Kings – the burial ground of Egypt's famous pharaoh kings.

The Valley of the Kings, or Wadi el Muluk in Arabic, has been known since the ancient royalty started burying their dead there, and many of the tombs were broken into and robbed of their treasures. However, quite a few tombs were quite well concealed, the most famous of which was King Tut's tomb discovered by Howard Carter in 1922.

We visited almost all tombs that were open and it was an awe-inspiring experience. With reverence for the buried Egyptian rulers, and amazement at the items they would need in the afterlife, what was remarkable to see were the chambers, intricately painted with brightly coloured images and hieroglyphs.

Luxor
Egypt

Luxor was the ancient city of Thebes, the great capital of Upper Egypt during the New Kingdom, and the glorious city of Amun, later to become the god Amun-Ra.

After our session at the University of Cairo and suitably briefed by an Egyptologist friend, Ma and me travelled to Luxor from Cairo in an overcrowded train. Steeped in history, an unhurried pace and friendly we fell in love with it instantly. Luxor is the world's greatest open-air museum, with well-preserved tombs, monuments, and temples. It's biggest draw, however, is that it is home to the tomb of the world-famous pharaoh Tutankhamun! The ancient city sits on the banks of the River Nile and is, undoubtedly, one of the most important archaeological sites in Egypt. It was a must-see on our Egypt itinerary, easily outshining Egypt's capital Cairo. We had a room with a view of the beautiful Nile. The heat in August was intolerable towards mid-day

and so we planned our trips quite early in the morning. The Valley of the Kings is an area of mountainous terrain, with over 60 tombs. Underground corridors, with incredible ancient wall-paintings, lead the way towards the tombs of some of the greatest Egyptian pharaohs.

The Colossi of Memnon are two massive 18-meter high stone statues, each carved from one single block of sandstone, battered for over 3,400 years by wind, sun, and water. But our favourite monument was the Karnak temple- the morning sunlight streamed over the massive columns, and hieroglyphs, of the majestic Karnak Temple that Friday! It is the world's second-largest religious complex, coming in closely behind Angor Wat in Cambodia . Dier el-Bahari. the enormous Temple of Queen Hatshepsut is a must-see in Luxor, ! The temple, set against a desert backdrop, is located near to the Valley of the Kings. Built from platforms and pillars, it has impressive sloping steps. We struggled up through the levels despite the heat but knew it was worth it once we reached the top. From the Nile cruise to browsing in antique stores, trying to read hieroglyphics to savouring local dishes, it was an unforgettable mother-daughter trip which will be treasured always.

UGANDA

When I was invited to present my paper at the World Conference on Women Studies at Makerere University, Kampala, Uganda, I was not very excited. Visiting a new university did excite me, but my usual rush of adrenaline at the slightest touch of wanderlust was missing. Little did I know that Uganda had its own secrets that would bedazzle the traveller in me. On the surface, Kampala is chaotic, dirty, confusing. Once you take the time to look beneath the surface, to really become friends with Kampala, you'll find a city that's truly alive, full of love and smiles and soul and laughter. And you, like myself, may find it very hard to leave.

Kampala is Uganda's national and commercial capital bordering Lake Victoria, Africa's largest lake. Hills covered with red-tile villas and trees surround an urban centre of contemporary skyscrapers. In this downtown area, the Uganda Museum explores the country's tribal heritage through an extensive collection of artefacts. On nearby Mengo Hill is Lubiri Palace, the former seat of the Buganda Kingdom.

The culture in Kampala is vibrant and varied. There is a big dance scene, particularly Latin dance, with salsa, kizomba and bachata nights (and free lessons) spread throughout the city almost every night of the week. Don't be shy — go and check it out! Zumba and yoga are growing in popularity and are not hard to find. I attended the annual Bayimba Arts Festival, which is centred around live music, crafts and dance, but the highlight was the stand-up comedy on offer, where some grassroots talent had the packed theatre roaring with laughs. As I would learn, stand-up has taken the city by storm, and for good reason.

The "Source of the Nile" was an unforgettable two hour tour to the historic Jinja Town, where the long and mighty river had its origin. Nile We had breakfast and lunch in the Mabira forest.

The mystic temples of Bagan

BAGAN

UNESCO World Heritage Site Mandalay Region

Sprawled on the banks of the Irrawaddy River, more than 3,000 temples stretch across a 30-square-mile plain in Bagan, Myanmar (formerly Burma) and nearby towns and villages. Constructed mostly between 1057 and 1287 by King Anawrahta, most temples are in ruins today. Bagan was the capital of the Kingdom of Pagan from the 9th to the 13th centuries. This kingdom was the first to unify the area that is now Myanmar, establishing the Burmese culture and ethnicity, and Theravada Buddhism in the region. Among the thousands of Pagodas are unaccountable, serene Buddha statues that cast a magic spell on the onlooker. Till today, many of these Buddhist monuments are revered. The living traditions are manifested by the festivals, celebrations and rituals performed by the locals, pilgrims and the monks

from the numerous monasteries. Presently rundown and in ruins, these priceless sentinels of history are in dire need of restoration. The main motivation for visiting Bagan for me, apart from the academic pursuit, was the authentic cultural experience. My sole satisfaction was from visiting the temples and pagodas, temple hopping like never before. I had a list of the must-see temples which I had to visit, but I could not resist getting down at almost every brick temple ruin that I came across. Gubyaukgyi temple with its amazing frescoes, Old Bagan, the ornamental tower of Hitlominlo Pahto, Kubyauk-gyi temple, near Myinkaba Village, walking trails, Irrawady nature walks, all this and much more are the memories I treasure!

Myanmar's Bagan showcases the largest concentration of Buddhist temples, pagodas and stupas in the world. The remains of over 2,500 monuments along with archaeological vestiges of ancient palaces, water management systems and fortifications are testimony to the highly evolved and significant Bagan period from the tenth to the thirteenth centuries CE. Exceptional architectural and artistic achievements are manifested in the exquisite ensembles of monuments with their intricate ornamentation and outstanding mural paintings. Till today, many of these Buddhist monuments are revered. The living traditions are manifested by the festivals, celebrations and rituals performed by the lo-

cals, pilgrims and the monks from the numerous monasteries. Presently rundown and in ruins, these priceless sentinels of history are in dire need of restoration. The main motivation for visiting Bagan for foreigners is the authentic cultural experience. Most tourists derive sole satisfaction from visiting the temples and pagodas. The large corpus of contemporary stone inscriptions has been the most reliable source for the history of the Kingdom. The mural paintings inside more than 300 temples constitutes a unique corpus of paintings of that time in southeast Asia.

    The uncountable number of temples that are spread across the plains of Bagan are the most impressive testament to the religious devotion of Myanmar's people – and rulers – over the centuries. They combine to form one of the richest archaeological sites in Asia and provide views quite unlike anywhere else on earth. The temples of Bagan constitute a World Heritage site.

The Irrawaddy River

There is an extraordinary timeless quality to Burma's Irrawaddy River, also known as the Ayeyarwady. The royalty of medieval Bagan valued the riverbank life: the bullock carts and ox-ploughs, the red-gold pagodas, rambling teak monasteries, and of course a view of the unmistakable Buddha statues. Our early morning walking tour along the Irrawaddy cleansed our minds deeply. With very few people around, we had the entire stretch of the elegantly meandering river all to ourselves. The refrains of Rilke's words echoed deep in me:

"May what I do flow from me like a river, no forcing and no holding back."

Though I visited several Pagodas, I shall write only about a few. The Nandamannya Pagoda in old Bagan (mid-13th century) is a single-chambered temple with fine frescoes and a ruined, seated Buddha image. Home to the forest dwelling monks, it was the seat of intense tantric rituals. One of the murals represents the 'temptation of Mara' episode in which nubile young females attempt to distract the Buddha from the meditation session that led to his enlightenment. I found it smaller than other pagodas and far less crowded.

The spectacular sunsets at Bagan

Scattered with poppies, the golden-green waves of the cornfields faded in the twilight. The red sun seemed to tip one end of a pair of scales below the horizon, and simultaneously to lift an orange moon at the other. The countless pagodas were awash with a reddish-gold hue that was sheer poetry. The clouds were like great wings of gold, yellow and rose-colour, with a sprinkle in one spot, like a shower of glowing stones from a volcano. Instantaneously, the hues would change to boundless masses of pink, and crimson, and scarlet, and purple, further up the dome of the sky. It made the scary climb along the narrow stairway up to the pagoda suddenly so worthwhile. Despite the teeming crowds, I find my own corner and my very own sunset.

"When the Bagan sun has set, no candle can replace it."

North Guni Temple
Bagan, Myanmar

Payanthonzu Temple

The Payathonzu Temple is a Buddhist temple located in the village of Minnanthu in Myanmar. It is unique in the sense that the temple consists of three temples conjoined through narrow passages. The walls of the corridors and the vaults are covered with beautifully painted and well preserved mural painting. The half decorated middle sanctum and the plain walls of the western temple indicate that the work was abandoned before completion.

"I am not the same, having seen the Bagan moon, lost amidst the poetry of temples..."

The Puppets of Bagan

Marionettes, string puppets, first became a form of entertainment in the royal court of Myanmar in the 1700's and the art form flourished for about a hundred years under royal patronage, until British colonization in 1885. It was revived in the late 1990's. Apparently it is as popular with the people of the country as it is with tourists.

Htilominlo Temple

Htilominlo is a Buddhist temple located in Bagan, in Burma/Myanmar, built during the reign of King Htilominlo, 1211-1231. The temple is three storeys tall, with a height of 46 metres, and built with red brick. Inside the 46-metre-high temple, which is similar in design to Sulamani Temple, there are four Buddha statues on the lower and upper floors. Traces of old murals are also still visible. Fragments of the original fine plaster carvings and glazed sandstone decorations have survived on the outside. The doorways

feature nice carved reliefs. Several old horoscopes, painted to protect the building from damage can be found on the walls of the temple. Each minute I spent there, I was aware of the utter stillness, the silence and the mystical past that was strewn all around!

Mahabodhi Temple

This is a Buddhist temple located in Bagan, Myanmar. It was built in the mid-13th century during the reign of King Htilominlo, and is modelled after the Mahabodhi Temple, which is located in Bihar, India. The temple is a two storey structure about 43 meters high. The pagoda and its square

base are stuccoed and contain depictions of several animals and Nat spirit figures. Both the lower and upper storey of the Mahabodhi temple contain a large seated Buddha image. On the inner wall is an inscription that provides information about the donation of the land where the temple was built on. The Mahabodhi temple was damaged during the earthquake of 1975, but has been restored since then.

Thanaka: the ancient Burmese beauty balm

Burmese traditional cosmetic, Thanaka, is used extensively by Burmese women to protect their skin and as a beauty balm. Thanaka means both 'Cosmetic for beauty' and 'cleansing' in Burmese and is used to protect the skin from sunlight.

It is made from roots and timber covers of Thanaka tree after an easy process, soaked in water and ground by a mortar. It is smooth, has a pleasant fragrance and is not only used daily but also for special events and festivals to reflect the aristocracy and social status of women.

I had this pattern drawn on my face by a beautiful young woman staying close to the Mahabodhi temple. I had seen it on many pretty Burmese faces and was eager to try it out. She sketched the pattern of a leaf on one cheek and said it would bring me luck. Wherever I went that day, I was showered with lot of affection by the Burmese people.

So much like the "Chandan", sandalwood patterns of Odisha & Bengal.

Philippines

Vacation with the Filipinos

MANILA

I visited Manila on an invitation from the Lyceum of the Phillipines University, Intramuros, Manila, Phillipines to present my paper at the 8th International Tourism Conference on "Asia Pacific Tourism: Innovations and Challenges in the age of m-Commerce". Frankly, 'Manila' had never conjured up the most positive images in my head. Invariably it brought up images of a city choked with traffic, ridden with crime and essentially a concrete jungle that is not known as the safest place in the world to travel. Government travel advisories and the well-publicised political challenges don't exactly restore one's faith in the city either.

It was an off-the-beaten-track trip for me. Manila, the capital of the Philippines, is a densely populated bay-side city on the island of Luzon, which mixes Spanish colonial architecture with modern skyscrapers. Intramuros, a walled city in colonial times, is the heart of Old Manila. It is home to the baroque 16th-century San Agustin Church as well as Fort Santiago, a storeyed citadel and former military prison. The city's name, originally Maynilad, is derived from that of the nilad plant, a flowering shrub adapted to marshy conditions, which once grew profusely along the banks of the river; the name was shortened first to Maynila and then to its present form. Architectural styles reflect American, Spanish, Chinese, and Malay influences.

We enjoyed our walk through Binondo, the commercial and dining destination is the oldest Chinatown in the world and home to some of the most expensive real estate in the Philippines. Across the Pasig River is Intramuros, the heart of Manila during Spanish colonial times; the walled city dates back to 1571 and is best explored by bicycle, preferably one made of bamboo. "Bambikes" are handmade by workers employed by Gawad Kalinga, a community-based development organisation working to bring an end to poverty.

From San Agustin Church, the oldest in the Philippines, to Manila Cathedral on to Fort Santiago. Built to prevent an invasion by sea, Fort Santiago was used as a barracks and a prison. In 1896, nationalist hero José Rizal spent two months incarcerated in the citadel before being marched to nearby Bagumbayan Field, where he was executed by firing squad. Renamed in his honour in 1967, Rizal Park is a soothing space of ornamental gardens, statues and fountains.

Manila has the world's worst traffic congestion, according to a study by GPS app Waze. The capital's chaos might be "charming" or "delightful" if you're in town for a day or two but for residents, it's energy sapping, irritating and stressful. Despite improving standards of living for some, the gaping disparity between rich and poor seems starker in Manila than in other developing countries; perhaps because it's one of the world's most densely populated cities.

Connecting to the past

CAMBODIA
Angkor Wat, Cambodia - connecting to the past.

With a rapidly evolving tourism scenario, the travelers motive to venture out has also undergone drastic change, ranging from varying motives for leisure to a need for the search for identity, to the search for creative and authentic experiences. It is widely acknowledged that travel plays an important part in shaping the perception of self through experiences of other people and places.

One of the evident consequences of tourism is defying the monotony of routine life and seeking out an "authentic" experience. Studies indicate that tourists are not only searching for the "Other", but are also on a quest for self-identity and that tourism is a vessel for self-discovery. Identity is essentially an individual notion. Regarding touristic experiences, "both remembering and forgetting also underlie a "subjective sense of identity" that is only inadequately reproduced in language.

Putting all of this together, an intense desire to unravel the unknown, roll under the canopy of stars and create my own world, all this has fueled my love for travel. From my childhood days I have always stretched my mind to touch new experiences. From adventure to sightseeing, destinations for music and dance, and of course, the fascination for temples, big and small, ancient and modern, the travel has continued.

Angkor Wat was identified as a World Heritage Site in 1992. The Angkor temple ruins, sprawling across the Unesco-protected Angkor archaeological park are the country's top tourist destination, with the main temple-city, Angkor Wat, appearing on the Cambodian national flag. Angkor (Khmer: "Capital City") was the capital city of Khmer Empire, which flourished from approximately 9th to 15th centuries. The ruins of Angkor are located amidst forests and farmland north of the Great Lake (Tonlé Sap) and south of the Kulen Hills, near modern-day Siem Reap city. The temples of the Angkor area number over one thousand, ranging in scale from nondescript piles of brick rubble scattered through rice fields to the Angkor Wat, said to be the world's largest single religious monument. Many of the temples at Angkor have been restored, and together, they comprise the most significant site of Khmer architecture. The entire expanse, including Angkor Wat and Angkor Thom is collectively protected as a UNESCO World Heritage Site. The popularity of the site among tourists presents multiple challenges to the preservation of the ruins.

The Angkorian period may have begun shortly after 800 AD, when the Khmer King Jayavarman II announced the independence of Kambujadesa (Cambodia) from Java and established his capital of Hariharalaya (now known as Roluos) at the northern end of Tonlé Sap. Through a series of military campaigns, alliances, marriages and land grants, he achieved a unification of the country bordered by China to the north, Champa (now Central Vietnam) to the east, the ocean to the south and a place identified by a stone inscription as "the land of cardamoms and mangoes" to the west. In 802, Jayavarman articulated his new status by declaring himself "universal monarch" (chakravartin) that linked him to the cult of Shiva, taking on the epithet of "god-king" (devaraja).

It was this interesting background of information that had me smitten and I had Angkor in my bucket list for a long time. So I set out for this trip with immense excitement. I was with a group of academicians for attending a conference at Siem Reap.

After arriving, as we glided through a sleepy, dusk-smeared Siem Reap, little did I know about the majestic spread of Angkor awaiting us. Travel blogs, books and websites have over-sold the destination. But nothing had prepared us for the regal beauty of Angkor. A sentinel of the past, it sprawled across acres of land, surrounded by a jungle of trees on all sides. I was awe-struck, silent, lost in my own thoughts. The landscape is identified by four main elements: tropical forest, cultivated land, scattered villages, and the cultural and architectural legacy of the Angkorean period.

As already seen in other temples, in various parts of

the world, the lions stood guard at the entry point. Cultural depictions of lions have been found in European, African and Asian countries. From Persia to Rome, the lion has been considered a symbol of the sun god Mithra, whilst the Etruscan lion with wings guards the entrance of the Temple Mountain at Troy. In Islam, Muhammad's son-in-law and cousin was referred to as the Lion of God, and a lion headed angel is one of four beings that supports Allah's throne.

The lion is also deeply ingrained in Buddhism, frequently pictured with bodhisattvas who guide people to the path of enlightenment, and Manjusri, a bodhisattva who is symbolic of transcendental wisdom is frequently on the back of a lion. The lion is not merely present across the major religions; it also suggests links or commonalities to the roots of many religions. For Jews, the lion is a symbol of messianic promise and redemption. This has parallels to both ancient civilizations and Christianity.

(http://lionalert.org/page/Lion_Depiction_Across_Ancient_and_Modern_Religions)

Angkor Wat as Mt. Meru:

What struck me most was the staggering size of Angkor, the earthly representation of Mt. Meru. An aerial view of Angkor Wat reveals the expansive enclosure wall of the temple, which separates the sacred temple grounds from the protective moat that surrounds the entire complex. The temple has three galleries (a passageway running along the length of the temple) with a central sanctuary, marked by five stone towers. The five stone towers are intended to symbolize the five mountain ranges of Mt. Meru—the mythical home of the gods, for both Hindus and Buddhists. The temple mountain as an architectural design was invented in Southeast Asia by architects who envisioned temples dedicated to Hindu gods on earth as a representation of Mt. Meru. The galleries and the empty spaces that they created between one another and the moat are envisioned as the mountain ranges and oceans that surround Mt. Meru. Mt. Meru is not only home to the gods, it is also considered an axis-mundi, a cosmic or world axis that connects heaven and earth. King Suryavarman II and his architects desired the temple to serve as the supreme abode for Vishnu. The anonymous temple architects, ingeniously designed the temple to reflect the cosmos (mandala) as well as a historical record of the temple's patron. (https://www.khanacademy.org/humanities/ap-art-history/south-east-se-asia/cambodia-art/a/angkor-wat)

In the Kings vying with each other to be better than their ancestors, Angkor rose to become the world's largest religious complex. I was fascinated by the many headed Nagas seen all over Cambodia, and at the entry point of Angkor, also, notably the naga balustrades. The fascinating apsaras, the quiet presence of Yogini- apsaras, the moat running all around all contributed to a delightful experience.

The amalgamation of Hindu iconography in this Buddhist kingdom was noticeable. Khmer adaptations of Ganesha and Hanuman were present all over the city, and both the *Ramayana* (known as the Reamker in Cambodia) and *Mahabharata* were significant in popular imagery. In Angkor Wat, Hindu deities, including a statue of Vishnu at the entrance now worshipped as a Buddhist shrine dominate.

Angkor Wat: A Mandala

The layout of Angkor Wat is arranged to make it one big sacred mandala. Designed as a symmetrical mandala, Angkor Wat has several correspondences in numbers and shapes. There are 108 lotus bud shaped towers, a sacred number to both Hindi and Buddhists. Mandala's were designed so that every proportion, space, area, ratio, length, breadth and height meant something deeper relating to Hindu cosmology. *A mandala is a spiritual and ritual symbol in Hinduism and Buddhism, representing the universe. In common* use, "mandala" has become a generic term for any diagram, chart or geometric pattern that represents the cosmos metaphysically or symbolically.

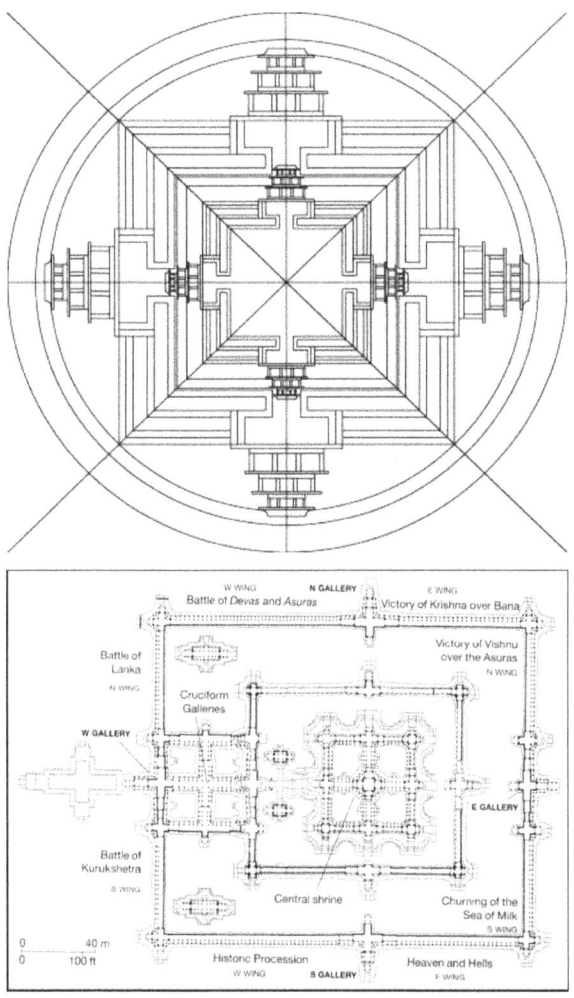

Angkor Wat is arranged around a series of mandala's interlinked to represent ever more complex cosmological and esoteric themes (world-mysteries.com/mystic-places/cambodias-)

Kalinga,(Odisha) had maritime ties with ancient Funan(Kambuja or modern Cambodia).The natives of Funan,called Khmers, believed that an Indian rishi was their ancestor. Around 500 CE, the Gangas of Kalinga(Eastern Gangas) were devotees of Siva-Gokarnaswami as the tutelary deity on Mahendra Mountain. Presently, too, there is the shrine of Gokarneswaraatop the hill. Worshipping of Gokarnaswami(on MahendraParvat in Kalinga) andMaheswara (in Funan) occurred at the same time.It was thus assumed that Funan was Indianized by the traders and merchants fromthe eastern coast of India, and with thepassage of time they named a local mountain of Funanas MahendraParvata after the MahendraParvata of Odisha. The famous Angkor-Wat ofCambodia has some affinities with the sikhara of the temples of Odisha and gopuras of the Tamil temples. In the BanteaySrei and Prah Khantemples of Cambodia, the mullioned openings arevery splendid and in their 'pattern and intention'areakin to the contemporary temples of Bhubaneswar in Odisha.

(P.Brown, India Architecture, (Buddhist and HinduPeriods), Bombay (Taraporevala Sons and Co.Pvt. Ltd.), 1971, p.184)

Drawn as I am, unfailingly, to the romance of ruins and old monuments, Angkor appealed to me almost like it was a primordial connection. As I saw it outlined against the pale morning sky, it was visually breath-taking, the stone lotus on top of the pyramid like temple. Such a colossal structure dedicated to the celebration of religion! Or was it the arrogance of Kings and monarchs to assume God-like images?

The big and small temples we saw ranged from beautiful structures like Angkor to brick rubbles in some places, Angkor Thom, almost falling apart to the

fascinating, tree infested Ta Prohm. Wherever we went we were struck by the architectural finesse of carvings inlaid in the walls- flowers, birds, animals, apsaras and yoginis. From King Solomon to most Indian Kings to the Khmer Kings, temples were unanimously seats of religious, sociocultural transactions. As we walked around the precincts of Angkor, I wondered how many footsteps of the past we were colliding with.

It was unbearably humid. So the temple's cool interior felt very pleasant. But we had a long day and many destinations to cover. So we had to venture out into the sun, sweaty, thirsty but nonetheless enriched by the visit. The stone steps leading to the different levels of Angkor can be strenuous, especially on a sunny day. We had been prepared for the attention of hawkers. Their language though unknown, the meaning was crystal clear. Life has to be lived forwards, but it's meaning lies unearthed in the past.

After the lunch that included corn pizza on site at Angkor Wat, we headed to the next destination, Bayon temples. This was smaller in size but also very uniquely

designed with faces carved on the outside of the temple. This is the only Angkorian state temple that was built primarily as a Mahayana Buddhist shrine dedicated to the Buddha, though a great number of minor and local deities are also present. Originally there were 54 towers, symbolizing the 54 provinces ruled by the king. However only 37 towers have stood the test of time and have been preserved. Each tower has four faces facing all directions, and the faces on each side are different. All towers were covered with gold. Besides the faces, of particular interest are the bas-reliefs, located in the galleries of the first and second tiers, more than 1,000 images of apsaras (celestial dancers). The temple was built in the spirit of Buddhism, despite unmistakable elements of Hinduism.

The next stop was the elephants terrace built by King Jayavarman VII towards the end of the 12th century. The terrace stretches out over a length of more than 300 meters from the Baphuon in the South to the Leper King terrace to the North. The terrace is unique for the sculptures in high relief of elephants and their mahouts. At several sections large elephant heads protrude out from the wall, their long trunks forming pillars extending to the ground. We slowly moved from the elephant terrace to a smaller complex where there were series of meditating buddhas on the wall.

Our visit to Ta Prohm was in the late afternoon. It was apparently built as a Mahayana Buddhist monastery and university. I was surprised by the massive invasion of the temple complex by plants mostly of silk cotton tree or banyans. It appeared that nature and architecture were locked in an eternal battle there. The sanctuary is built around the huge, elevated stone face of Prajnaparamita, the personification of wisdom, whose features were modelled after those of the king's mother. Ta Prohm's popularity has

soared in recent years along with the rest of the Angkor complex, but especially because of its appearance in the movie *Lara Croft: Tomb Raider*.

The roots which obviously started as tender cellular

elements soon spread their structure over the temple walls. There were some sites inside the complex with Buddha worship. By the time we were done there it was almost evening.

The day after was a bright sunny journey. The Bayon or Face temple with its smiling faces sculpted on all sides was a wonder for us. Despite the merciless Sun beating down on us, we revelled in the grandeur. The faces were intriguing in their timelessness. The meaning of these faces

now remains a debate. Some say they embody the image of the great Angkor King, King Jayavarman VII, who built Bayon temple. It is said that he wanted to create these faces to dedicate to Buddha. Another belief is that these faces belonged to the *bodhisattva* (Buddhist enlightened being) of compassion known as Avalokiteśvara. There's another theory suggesting that both of the aforementioned hypotheses are partially true as King Jayavarman identified himself with Buddha and *bodhisattva*.

It saddened us to see the heaps of rubble lying as remnants of beautiful temples, stone temples rolling helplessly on that historic soil. From gates decorated with elephant trunks, Gods and demons, faces of Avalokiteshwar, we were mesmerized by all we saw. As the temple was built in several layers, we had to do a lot of climbing up and down. Life size Buddha statues on the outside of the temple led to the Elephant terrace. King Jayavarman's viewing platform became ours that day, for those moments we were there. Where he looked at the return of his victorious armies, we looked at each other and undeniably agreed that we had the better option to the terrace of the leper king.

Engulfed as I am in my continuing research on the Yogini cult of India, I looked for the existence of a Yogini trail at Angkor as well. The inscriptions of the images of goddesses on the walls, nooks and corners of Angkor has been a topic of considerable debate. There is not much information available on who these women of Angkor Wat were and what principles of spirituality they represent.

Each female portrait at Angkor Wat is distinctly different, with unique varieties in their pose, hand positions (mudras), ethnicity, jewellery, clothing, hair style, accoutrements and location. (Kent Davis)

*Angkor Wat devata from the bakkan,
the sacred level of the temple. Photo: Kent Davis*

In a world that is increasingly connected through travel, leisure being redefined as doing what one wishes to, Angkor meets various needs of tourists. From historians to researchers, the sight-seeing groups to religious seekers, Angkor is the place where religion meets spirituality, where the past meets the present.

Malaysia

A trip to Paradise

LANGKAWI ISLAND

Some 30 km off the west coast of mainland Malaysia lies an archipelago of over 100 islands amidst the turquoise waters of the Andaman Sea - the Langkawi groups of islands, coveted as the Jewel of Kedah. With us were travellers of all kinds – nature lovers, history buffs, adventure seekers, and even mad romantics. Langkawi islands offers something for all.

The main Langkawi island itself is known for its marvellous diving opportunities. From the stretches of the magnificent beach to the Cable Car in Pantai Kok, Langkawi continues to provide a new delight in every minute fragment. Our hotel was idyllic, the Mutiara Burau Bay Beach Resort, surrounded by untouched coastal rainforests and located along two of Langkawi's beaches, Pantai Kok and Burau Bay. The forests are home to a rich and varied wildlife. We were delighted to spot many squirrels, lizards and birds as they roamed the extensive landscaped gardens next to our nature cottage.

We visited the Eagle Square, also known as Dataran Lang, one of Langkawi's best known man-made attractions, a large sculpture of an eagle poised to take flight. A sight that greets visitors to the island via ferry, the 12meter-tall statue is one of the island's most instantly recognizable monuments. The island is especially recognised for its mangrove swamps, neighbouring islets and thriving coral system, so island-hopping and mangrove tours are readily available all year long. We took a boat for our group with a guide. We had a quick visit to the bat caves, which is close to the mangrove swamp walk, followed by a visit to the crocodile cave, and fish farm which was really really fun!!! Then a visit to the other side of the river where different species of eagles live and finally a tour out to the Andaman sea, with very interesting story telling by our expert guide made it a worthwhile experience

Finally, no holiday in Langkawi is complete without sampling local seafood dishes which we did and truly enjoyed.

When the ruins speak

YOGYAKARTA

Borobudur Temple,
Java, Indonesia

Borobudur, or Barabudur, is a 9th-century Mahayana Buddhist Temple in Magelang, Central Java, Indonesia. The monument consists of nine stacked platforms, six square and three circular, topped by a central dome. Built in three tiers: a pyramidal base with five concentric square terraces, the trunk of a cone with three circular platforms and, at the top, a monumental stupa. This famous Buddhist temple, dating from the 8th and 9th centuries, is located in central Java. It was built in three tiers: a pyramidal base with five concentric square terraces, the trunk of a cone with three circular platforms and, at the top, a monumental stupa. The walls and balustrades are decorated with fine low reliefs, covering a total surface area of 2,500 m2. Around the

circular platforms are 72 openwork stupas, each containing a statue of the Buddha. The monument was restored with UNESCO's help in the 1970s. Visiting Borobudur was a "dream come true" experience for me and the primary reason why I had decided to visit Java. In my previous visit to Indonesia, I had travelled to Jakarta and Bandung as a member of a delegate of tourism professionals earlier. Jakarta was just a stopover for me but I stayed a day to go around this big city. A visit to the National Museum, mosques and cathedrals had been the high-point of that busy day. But Yogyakarta was where I longed to be.

I spent many special moments at Ratu Boko, Universitas Gadjah Mada and the indomitable Mount Merapi, Yogyakarta,Indonesia . Standing majestically on a hillside plateau overlooking the magnificent Prambanan temples and the mystical Mount Merapi as its backdrop, the Ratu Boko Palace ruins are the remnants from the glorious 8th century golden age of ancient Javanese kingdoms. I did not travel to Yogyakarta (popularly referred to as Jogja) as a backpacker but as a cultural tourist, to unravel its miraculous inheritance of Borobudur and Prambanan temples. While there, I got to mingle with a group of backpackers from different parts of Europe and US. Most of them were in their thirties, avid travelers and in search of spiritual enlightenment. This spurred my interest to study the backpackers travel trends. The experience is of utmost importance: I found the group sharing personal experiences connected with the need to self-actualize by the travel to Borobudur.

- The historical heritage became the perfect backdrop for accentuating the need for creating an identity. many philosophical questions were discussed on the topmost platform of Borobudur, with the life-size Buddha statues as the only witness.

- To see the most within the constraints of budget.: The spirit of the group was indefatigable. They wanted to see every bit of the temple complex of Prambanan nad Borobudur. From the rare sight of sunrise atop the hill Bukit Punthuk Setumbu, to exploring every plaque in every level of Borobudur, the steep climb up all temples of Prambanan to watching the Ramayan theatre group, everything was part of the "must do" list.
- Assimilation with the local culture, cuisine and people: Being in the heartland of Javanese culture left us with no option but to try out everything that the local culture offered- watching the classical music and dance show at the The Kraton Ngayogyokarto Hadiningrat (the Sultan's Palace), exploring the batik bazaar, traditional crafts, and trying out the traditional dishes (Gudeg,Gado Gado, Kupat Sayur, the list is endless) at wayside restaurants.
- Entertainment and thrill: I found the group of backpackers very open to new adventure, from unknown hiking trails to scaling Mt.Merapi.
- Enhanced social skills: Not only did the group communicate with each other but easily mingled with the locals as well. It brings to an end the prejudice that cultural stereotypes can at times create. Forging new friendships, facing crisis, dealing with stress and cross-cultural issues all make the backpacker a well-rounded personality with a meaning ful social network.

Kraton Ratu Boko

Ratu Boko is popularly called Kraton Ratu Boko. It was once a palace for Ratu Boko, the father of Lara

Jonggrang. It was built during the 8th century AD by the Buddhist Sailendra Dynasty, and later, the Hindu Mataram kings took over the place. This take over rendered Kraton Ratu Boko replete with Hindu and Buddhist references. Inscriptions indicate that the palace initially was named "Abhayagiri Vihara" - which literally means "monastery on a peaceful hill," indicating that it was built for seclusion and focused on spiritual life.

All over Ratu Boko, visitors can find both Hindu and Buddhist symbols. These reveal that the two religions co-existed peacefully in ancient Java. The site covers 16 hectares spread over two hamlets (Dawung and Sambireja). In contrast to other Classic-period sites in Central Java and Yogyakarta, which are remains of temples, Ratu Boko reflects features of a settlement. Seemingly a palace complex belonging to the kings of Sailendra or Mataram Kingdom that also built temples across the Prambanan Plain, Ratu Boko site consists of seven parts of the complex building. Abhayagiri Vihara inscription dated 792 CE is one of the few written evidence discovered in Ratu Boko site. Some Hindu elements are also found at the site, such as the discovery of statues of Hindu deities: Durga, Ganesha and Yoni.

In many ways, visiting Indonesia was like homecoming for me. Yogyakarta, Java's cultural soul appealed to me instantly. The memories I have collected gleam in my mind like diamonds. I lost sight of the shore in that mystic land, only to discover an ocean in me!

◻

Black Eagle Books

www.blackeaglebooks.org
info@blackeaglebooks.org

Black Eagle Books, an independent publisher, was founded as a nonprofit organization in April, 2019. It is our mission to connect and engage the Indian diaspora and the world at large with the best of works of world literature published on a collaborative platform, with special emphasis on foregrounding Contemporary Classics and New Writing.

www.ingramcontent.com/pod-product-compliance
Lightning Source LLC
Chambersburg PA
CBHW061208070526
44583CB00025B/3163